# AFRICAN ELEPHANTS

## A Celebration of Majesty

DEDICATION

FOR OUR MOTHERS, JOY AND MO, TWO VERY SPECIAL MATRIARCHS;
AND FOR TSHOKWANE, WHO LET ME LIVE.

# AFRICAN ELEPHANTS

## A Celebration of Majesty

### DARYL AND SHARNA BALFOUR

FOREWORDS BY
DR IAIN DOUGLAS-HAMILTON,
DR JOHN HANKS AND DAPHNE SHELDRICK

STRUIK PUBLISHERS (PTY) LTD
(A MEMBER OF THE STRUIK PUBLISHING GROUP (PTY) LTD)
CORNELIS STRUIK HOUSE, 80 McKENZIE STREET
CAPE TOWN 8001

REG. NO.: 54/00965/07

MANAGING EDITOR: MARJE HEMP
DESIGN AND DTP: JANICE EVANS
EDITOR: DONALD REID
DESIGN ASSISTANT: LELLYN CREAMER
CARTOGRAPHY: CAROLINE BOWIE
TOPOGRAPHY: MOUNTAIN HIGH MAPS TM COPYRIGHT © 1993 DIGITAL WISDOM, INC.
ILLUSTRATION IN 'TRAMPLED BY TSHOKWANE': PHILIP HUEBSCH
ILLUSTRATION FOR CHAPTER OPENERS: DAVID THORPE

REPRODUCTION BY CMYK PREPRESS, CAPE TOWN
PRINTED AND BOUND IN SINGAPORE BY TIEN WAH PRESS (PTE) LTD

*FRONTISPIECE: One of Kruger National Park's large tuskers, the last of the really big ivory carriers on the African continent.*

*TITLE PAGE: A large breeding herd mills about defensively, their youngsters safely secured among the adults, after being surprised in open ground in Tarangire National Park.*

*RIGHT: Amboseli is home to some of the most studied elephants in Africa, such as this distinctive cow known as Echo by the Amboseli Elephant Research Project.*

*OVERLEAF: Namibia's desert-adapted elephants – reputed to be the tallest in the world – are nevertheless dwarfed by the vast and desolate landscape.*

# CONTENTS

# AUTHORS' PREFACE

This book represents not only a personal record of a four-year odyssey spent following and living with elephants in some of the more remote areas of Africa, but also a pictorial tribute to a magnificent creature that we feel embodies the very essence of wilderness. *African Elephants – A Celebration of Majesty* reflects some of our experiences and highlights some of the issues facing elephants and those entrusted with their conservation today. We are not scientists, so we have avoided trying to present a comprehensive biological or behavioural treatise. Rather we have shared our personal visions and attempted to distil almost four years of photographic experiences across Africa into a book which we hope will inspire the same feelings of love, wonder, awe and respect we came to feel for our subjects.

When we started this undertaking we envisaged it as a year-long project. We intended spending no more than several months in South Africa's Kruger National Park photographing its legendary big tuskers, gathering a portfolio to supplement our existing elephant material from parks and places already visited in Namibia and Botswana. The book was intended to reflect a southern African conservation success story as opposed to the disastrous tales we were hearing about poaching and the decimation of elephant herds further north. But, as our time among the elephants lengthened and we learned more about our subjects and matters affecting their lives, we realised that we needed to broaden our own horizons, as well as the scope of our research and photography. First we travelled to Zimbabwe, then spent much more time in both Botswana and Namibia. We drove north, through Zambia, Malawi and Tanzania

The challenge that lies ahead is to manage the earth's remaining resources for the future benefit of not only all mankind, but animal – and elephant – kind too. To preserve the land in all its diversity for the inhabitants of Planet Earth we will have to embark upon some far-sighted management of our own species, for undoubtedly man's own unchecked population growth presents the greatest threat to the future survival of all earth's species. Africa – and the world – will surely be a poorer place if these magnificent behemoths can no longer tread their ancient footpaths.

to Kenya, where our eyes were opened beyond our wildest expectations. Despite all that we had heard and been told, here we found some of the happiest elephants in Africa, and enjoyed some of our most memorable times among them. In Amboseli National Park in Kenya, at the foot of Mount Kilimanjaro, a baby elephant, only a few weeks old, leant up against our vehicle and slept peacefully while its unconcerned mother ate a trunk's length away.

Our experience with Kenya's elephants, which meet with minimal interference from man, was humbling and soul-cleansing, and made us search deep in our hearts and minds to begin a reassessment of policies and principles which we'd (almost) come to accept.

Isolated through the apartheid years at the southern tip of the continent, perhaps South Africa's 'successes' in managing its elephant population needed re-examination. In this computerised, super-efficient world of ours, perhaps we'd be well advised not to let slip a few old-fashioned concepts like morality and ethics in our dealings with and about our fellow inhabitants of this planet.

The facts are that at the turn of this century there were an estimated 10-million elephants in Africa. In 1979 Kenya-based biologist and elephant researcher Dr Iain Douglas-Hamilton, in the first really extensive continental census of elephant populations conducted for the International Union for the Conservation of Nature (IUCN), calculated that there was a total of 1,43 million elephants left on the continent. Ten years later that figure had been slashed by more than half and numbers were down to about 609 000, decimated by the effects of illegal ivory hunting and the insidious loss of elephant range. Today, thanks to the 1989 decision banning the international trade in elephant products, the slide to extinction has been slowed – but not yet stopped, let alone reversed.

There are, however, many people who would say that half a million elephants is enough – too many even; that elephants living outside national parks and game reserves have no place in today's world. Indeed, for those who have to live with them under uncontrolled conditions, elephants are nothing more, or less, than a serious nuisance and a real threat to life, limb and property. To many rural Africans living in close proximity to wildlife areas, the only good elephant is a dead one, and it's hard to argue with such logic when one small herd of elephants can devastate a year's crops – and a family's livelihood – in a night, destroy a homestead and (as they can and frequently do) cripple, maim or kill family or friends. While the average Westerner, living in Johannesburg, London, New York, Berlin or any other big city and unlikely ever to experience such life and death conflicts with animals, may be aghast at such sentiments,

it is not easy to counter them, fuelled as they are by the practicalities of a hard life, under difficult conditions on a harsh continent. As the months lengthened into years, what started for us as a simple project grew into a labour of love as curious affection became committed passion. We feel greatly privileged to have been afforded the opportunity to share in the lives of so many of Africa's remaining elephants, and trust we can encourage more people to visit them in the reserves where they live. The pleasure of lying at night in a tent in the African wilderness, listening to the rumbling of wild elephants, is a simple reminder of man's own valuable but everdiminishing freedom. Elephants, sensitive and intelligent creatures, are more than mere numbers, and if they need to be managed this should be done with a modicum of sensitivity and understanding – and without resort to bloody carnage associated with culling.

*An elephant feeds peacefully on the shores of Zimbabwe's Lake Kariba, apparently unaware of the threats facing its future.*

# TRAMPLED BY TSHOKWANE

The elephant was a scant 30 metres away, feeding greedily on the new leaves that had appeared on the scrubby acacia after the first rains of summer a few weeks previously. His back to me, he was oblivious to my presence as I stood staring at the long, smooth, creamy tusks that shone dully in the early morning sun, their full length hidden by the foliage that reached halfway up his body. If this was Tshokwane, second only to the magnificent Mandleve in tusk size and weight and thus probably the second largest tusker alive in Africa, then we'd be home for Christmas, an eight-month task searching for and photographing the legendary big bull elephants of Kruger National Park finally complete. I just needed to confirm his identity, and to do that I had to get a clear, frontal view of him.

We had left Tshokwane to last because much of his range fell within the Sweni wilderness trails area and we had been asked by the park authorities to avoid the area while the trails season was in full swing. Early on December 3, the last day of the season, we visited section ranger Jack Greef at his Nwanetsi outpost. After we had explained our mission, Jack enthusiastically pointed out on our map the area where he'd seen the huge elephant a few days previously, and gave us the all-clear to enter the trails area that morning.

It was about 8.30am when we first saw an elephant about one or two kilometres off the road south of Nwanetsi camp, but, even by standing on the roof of our four-wheel-drive vehicle and scanning the dense bush with binoculars, we couldn't be sure if it was our quarry. It was a big tusker all right, and so I decided to walk towards him for a closer look, leaving Sharna, who had broken her spectacles a few days earlier, with the vehicle. As I set off she called out to me to fetch her if the elephant was indeed Tshokwane.

As I entered the area of acacia thornscrub where the elephant was feeding I made sure I stayed downwind of him as I manoeuvred into a good position to get some shots. The sun coming over my left shoulder lit the magnificent elephant perfectly and, hoping he would turn towards me as he fed, I waited patiently for some time. Then he started moving deeper into the thornscrub, out of view, and I decided to try to attract his attention. Softly I clicked my gold wedding band on the aluminium leg of my tripod.

The elephant spun around on the spot, ears flared wide to pick up the source of the alien sound. Catching sight of me, he raised his head as he drew himself up into a typical, threatening, 'standing tall' posture.

'Tshokwane, you beauty!' I breathed excitedly, recognising his magnificent tusks as they came into full view. I focused and began shooting, the click and whirr of the camera the only sound breaking the silence of the morning. Then he charged . . .

'Wonderful shots!' I said to myself, refocusing and zooming out as the towering elephant bore down on me. From past experiences with countless other elephants, I was familiar with the characteristics of a mock charge and all the attempts at intimidation – drawing himself up to his full height, ears flared, trunk tossing and flailing in my direction, stopping every few strides to kick dust and leaves at me. Impressive – and terrifying if you don't recognise the bluff! I carried on shooting until he skidded to a standstill about six or seven metres away. It was a standoff, and time stood still as neither of us backed down. Previous encounters had also taught me to stand my ground when faced with a mock charge, and over the years I'd grown confident of my ability to differentiate between bluff and deadly intent. But now, sensing the elephant's uncertainty, and becoming acutely aware of a rising concern of my own, I raised myself up and threw my arms into the air, shoo-ing the towering elephant off. Simultaneously, Tshokwane and I turned away from our confrontation, both of us retreating with a sense of uncertainty and relief. Walking away steadily, I watched as the magnificent bull moved off, head high, tail erect, keeping an eye on me over his shoulder as he returned to the acacia thicket.

*Tshokwane charges with deadly intent! Seconds after the shutter clicked, I turned to run, in vain ... This photograph was one of the final exposures on the roll of film recovered from my battered camera after the trampling.*

It had been a tense moment, and I breathed deeply as I brought my adrenalin-induced shakes under control. But what a spectacular animal he was! I picked up my pace, heading back to the road to tell Sharna that I'd found Tshokwane.

I'd gone a hundred metres or so when I stopped to look back, making sure that I'd be able to retrace my steps with Sharna. Then my photographic instinct rose within me again – Tshokwane had gone back to feeding, side-on in a cluster of fresh, green, newly sprouted acacia, the light was perfect and he stood at the far side of a small, open patch in the scrub. 'Let me get a few more shots,' I thought, 'the setting is better, this light won't hold and, by the time we return, he could have moved into the thick stuff again.' I turned back, mounting a different lens on the Nikon and making sure that my second camera was at the ready.

I approached slowly and carefully, and could see that Tshokwane was aware of my presence, although he continued feeding normally. As long as I make sure I don't encroach on his 'flight zone' and chase him away – or provoke another charge – I'll get some superb shots, I told myself, cautiously picking through a dense stand of thorn-bush to the edge of the clearing. Breaking out into the open, I immediately bent over into a stooped 'baboon walk', chose a good position and squatted on the ground. My tripod was set to its lowest position, and I hunched over the camera to focus on the elephant, who was still feeding some distance away.

Suddenly, without any warning, Tshokwane turned and charged. Bursting from where he fed out into the clearing, he came at me once again, still with the tall, shuffling gait of the mock charge. I didn't move, concentrating on the photography, and felt momentary relief when he stopped in a cloud of dust about 15 metres away. Quickly I swopped cameras to a shorter lens.

Then, with chilling fury, he trumpeted in rage, lowered his head, and came on. I had taken a few more shots before realisation struck.

'This is for real! He's not going to stop.' I scrambled to my feet, scooped up the tripod and turned to run, knowing it was too late . . . Thereafter my memories are a blur. I'd gone only a few paces when Tshokwane's trunk hit me low in my back, the first blow deceptively light. I thought, momentarily, 'That's all he's going to do!' The second blow knocked me flying, and I tumbled through the sharp thorns. Before I had a chance to gather my wits or attempt to roll clear, the elephant was upon me, kicking, stomping and flailing with massive feet and legs. It was a moment of sheer terror, followed by mayhem and madness. My only thought was of survival, as I desperately tried to keep out from under those deadly feet.

'Clinch, get into a clinch,' some long-ago boxing lesson told me and I flung my arms around one huge leg, pulling myself into as small a bundle as I could manage. The rough, abrasive hide of Tshokwane's legs, like coarse-grade sandpaper, rasped skin off my arms and face, yet all I remember thinking at the time was how funny the spiky little black hairs on his leg looked, and that the elephant's black toenails were the ugliest things I'd ever seen.

Perhaps grabbing hold of the elephant's foreleg like that, almost like going on the offensive, took him by surprise, but Tshokwane stilled momentarily, then stepped back and to the side. One of his feet came down on my left calf and I screamed in agony. Then quite casually he reached down with his trunk, curled it around my right leg below the knee and plucked me out from under him. My already weakened grip was no match for the huge elephant's power and I felt myself swinging in a graceful arc through the air.

I smashed to the ground with a sickening thud that knocked the breath from my chest and sent blinding pain coursing through what remained of my consciousness as my hip dislocated. Now writhing on the brink of oblivion, I looked up, my vision blurred by dirt, dust and sheer bloody pain, and saw Tshokwane's tusks bearing down on me. At the last moment I wrenched myself to one side, but took a glancing blow from a tusk on the side of my head behind the right ear – a hit that knocked me senseless and possibly saved my life.

My tattered and bloody body limp and apparently lifeless, Tshokwane possibly thought he had killed me. Rangers and trackers who subsequently interpreted the spoor and battle-signs in the dirt believed that the enraged bull had attempted to deliver the *coup de grâce* by kneeling to crush my unconscious form, in the manner in which elephants typically finish off their victims. Tshokwane's long tusks, however, prevented him from getting down on to his knees and, despite apparently making several attempts – there were numerous gouge marks in the earth where his tusks left deep scars – and kicking and rolling my body in the dirt, he was unsuccessful and eventually must have left my inert form for dead.

I, however, still like to believe he knowingly left me alive – that he let me live, for he had many other means at his disposal and could have killed me had he really wanted to.

Sharna meanwhile was oblivious to the drama unfolding only a kilometre or two from the vehicle. Here she takes up the story:

'Daryl had been gone for slightly longer than I expected, and after an hour and a half I started feeling slightly uneasy. I scanned the bush with my binoculars, but there was no sign of him or the elephant, and I didn't want to go looking for him in case I spoiled his photo-shoot. So I carried on reading my book, looking up every now and then in the hope that I'd see him walking back towards me.

Suddenly I heard a shot, followed by two more, evenly spaced apart – a distress signal Daryl had often discussed with me – and I knew, instinctively, that he'd been trampled. He would never fire his gun in the bush unless he was in serious distress, and I immediately drove off the track into the bush, trying to recall the direction he'd walked and heading towards the gunshots.

Soon I got into thick bush and I could barely see a few metres ahead of me. I was driving round in circles, pressing on the hooter and shouting his name out the window. At one stage I stopped and climbed up on the roof of the vehicle, calling out to him all the time. Then more gunshots split the air, one buzzing dangerously past me, and I realised that he was less than a hundred metres away. I jumped down, climbed back into the cab and proceeded to crash the vehicle through the bush. I came into a small clearing and saw him where he had dragged himself into the shade under a small thornbush and was calling weakly, barely conscious.

He looked absolutely ghastly. Blood and dirt had combined to a gory mud that caked his abrasions and grossly swollen calf, and I could see his hip was at a terrible, unnatural angle. He was desperately thirsty and obviously wracked with pain, yet as I drove up he gestured feebly for me to stop, and called out to be careful I didn't drive over his cameras! The elephant had smashed them to bits, and pieces were scattered all around the battlefield – I didn't think there'd be much worth salvaging there, but I did what he asked anyway.'

When I slowly began to regain consciousness I was surprisingly aware of my situation. I knew that my hip was badly dislocated and that my left calf was the size of a football where the elephant had crushed it underfoot. There was no way I was getting out of there alone! I usually seek permission from park authorities to conduct my research and photography on foot, and usually a precondition of this permit is that I carry a firearm. Although I decided way back at the beginning of my career as a wildlife photographer that I would never use a gun to defend myself against an animal which I had knowingly put myself at risk with, I carried a revolver in a holster around my waist. Sharna and I had frequently discussed the possibility that one day I may slip and injure myself or suffer a snake bite, and that in such an eventuality, should I be alone, I would signal by firing three shots in the air.

However, when I reached for my holster the revolver wasn't there. Tshokwane had wrenched a camera bag and the heavy leather holster from my belt, but fortunately the clasp holding the gun had come undone in the turmoil, and when the holster was tossed aside the revolver fell free. Looking around where I lay in the dust, I saw the gleaming metal a few metres away. Painfully, centimetre by agonising centimetre, I dragged myself towards it. A few times I fought back as unconsciousness threatened to sweep over me again. I knew I had to summon help, or die under the blazing mid-summer sun.

Eventually I reached out and gripped the barrel of the gun, raised it over my head and fired the three shots I knew would bring Sharna to my side. I then dragged myself another metre into the shade under a low thornbush, and passed out once again.

Sometime later I regained consciousness, consumed by desperate thirst, my mouth and nose filled with soil and dust. Finding myself alone still, I fired the gun again. What seemed seemed like hours later, but was in fact was only minutes, I saw our four-wheel drive advancing through the brush and then, through a crimson haze, Sharna running to my side. . . .

'I knew I had to get Daryl to hospital immediately, but I didn't know if I'd be able to lift him or if I might aggravate unseen injuries, and I thought about making him comfortable and going to find help. Then I remembered the remains of a kill we had seen not far up the road, with hyaenas and vultures in attendance. I knew I had to get him into the truck myself and, guessing he had no serious spinal injuries from the way he was able to move his upper body, decided then to take the risk.

Fortunately we had a number of rigid camera cases in the back of the vehicle, so I reversed as close as I could to where Daryl lay, then arranged the cases to make a series of steps. Then, coaxing him to help me by lifting and pulling with his arms, which apart from minor cuts, deep abrasions and sharp thorns, were not injured, I got him up on to the first step. Each movement brought gut-wrenching groans from Daryl, but step by step together we managed to get him up into the back of the vehicle. There, fortunately, we had a mattress he could lie on, although the extent and severity of his injuries meant that he was far from comfortable .

Then I couldn't find my way back out of the dense bush to the road! Daryl, vaguely conscious, suggested I get out, see where the

*BELOW: Tshokwane in the bull elephant's typical threat posture – ears spread wide and head held high, attempting to appear as imposing as possible.*

*OVERLEAF: Two large bulls go through an elaborate greeting ritual. Younger elephants and those inferior in status will reach out with their trunks in salute, frequently even inserting the tip into the senior elephant's mouth.*

sun was, and head toward it, as he knew he'd walked due west when he'd left the road. But by now it was close to midday and the sun was overhead. Eventually, by getting out and walking ahead for a few metres, returning to the car, edging forward, then getting out again, I followed my tracks to the road, then set off at high speed for the park headquarters at Skukuza. I knew I would have to get fuel there before continuing to the nearest hospital in the town of Nelspruit, about a two hour drive further on.

The journey was a nightmare. I usually have to wear my glasses to drive, and I was terrified an animal would step into the road and we'd have an accident. I was praying that a traffic officer would step

out to pull me over for speeding so that I could get him to drive, all the while trying to talk to Daryl in the back to stop him relapsing into unconsciousness. It was only when I was busy filling up with fuel at Skukuza that I remembered there was a resident doctor in the camp. I ran inside and blurted out what had happened.'

Dr. Johan Ferreira had seen a few elephant victims in his years as Kruger Park doctor but, he told me later, they were all corpses. When he found me, battered and bloodied in the back of our pickup, he believed he had another on his hands. With a blood pressure down to a critical 60/40, he feared I had massive internal haemorrhaging. It was imperative, he knew, that he stabilise me and get me to hospital as soon as possible. Treating me where I lay in the back of the pick-up, Dr. Ferreira set up drips to stabilise my condition and administered welcome painkillers while his assistant summoned the NPB's helicopter – fortunately not in use elsewhere in the park that day. Soon it clattered overhead and landed nearby, and I was loaded on to a stretcher and manoeuvered inside. With the pilot, Dr. Ferreira and me aboard there was no room for Sharna and, standing in the crowd that had been attracted by the arrival of the helicopter, she listened as several of those who'd helped load the stretcher remarked that I wouldn't make it, that I would be dead on arrival.

The agonising 40-minute flight to hospital in Nelspruit passed in a blur. Gritting my teeth, I tried to crack jokes with the pilot and reassure the doctor I was not about to die! I drifted semi-consciously in a sea of pain, until we landed and the relief of anaesthetic oblivion came at the hospital.

I awoke some time later. It was dark outside and Sharna, her family, and Schalk and Loretta van der Sandt, friends who worked in Kruger and who had rushed to the hospital as soon as they heard, were at the bedside. The pain was almost gone, and there were swathes of bandages around my arms and legs. My right hip was dislocated and the leg was in traction, I had numerous fractured ribs, a slight fracture of the skull where one of the tusks had hit my head, a sprained ankle, a badly bruised calf and countless bruises and abrasions all over my body . . . but, miraculously, I was alive. I smiled weakly and called to Sharna's father, 'I got some great shots.'

I closed my eyes, ready to drift off again, then opened them with a start. Sharna leaned closer and gripped my hand in hers.

'Don't let them shoot Tshokwane, please don't let them shoot him,' I murmured to her, 'it was all my own fault.'

## POSTSCRIPT

Tshokwane was marked down to be destroyed during the 1995 culling operation, along with a number of other bulls that had shown aggression towards tourist vehicles or people on guided walking trails, though thankfully this didn't take place. I do not believe his attack on me was the cause of his aggression, as has been argued, but rather that the attack was a symptom of his growing intolerance of the presence of human beings over the years.

I realise that I made an error of judgment in returning for the 'second round' of photography, and almost paid the ultimate price. Had I simply continued walking back to the road that morning I undoubtedly would not carry the various scars I do today. But professional photography is a competitive field and risk-taking is inherent to the job, as evidenced by the number of cameramen who have fallen in riot-torn townships, battlefields and war-zones around the globe. Sharna herself almost died as a result of malaria contracted in Kenya while researching this book – just another of the hazards of the profession!

It took four months before I was back on my feet without assistance and able to return to Kruger. I was determined to find Tshokwane and let him see me alive . . . I was certain he'd let me live when he could so easily have finished me off.

We returned to the scene of the incident and walked around, pondering over the dramatic incident that had taken place here. The scars in the earth had gone, covered by heavy summer rains and fresh growth, and so had Tshokwane, off somewhere in the bushveld.

One of the first people I talked to on my return to the park was the experienced young trails ranger Steven Whitfield, who regularly led walking trails in the Sweni area and had often provided me with useful information about Tshokwane's whereabouts and movements during the time we spent in the Kruger Park.

'Has Tshokwane ever been aggressive in the past?' I asked him, curious because all my encounters with other venerable old tuskers had been very 'gentlemanly'.

'Oh yes,' Steven responded, 'he's never liked people!'

'Thanks for warning me,' I replied. 'Perhaps it's just as well I didn't find him again!'

Maybe it was for the best that we didn't meet a second time, though I still like to believe he may have raised his trunk to test the wind, a greeting perhaps. . . .

# FOREWORD BY DR IAIN DOUGLAS-HAMILTON

## AN EAST AFRICAN PERSPECTIVE

In this book Daryl and Sharna Balfour share with us their personal vision of a creature they feel embodies the very essence and wonder of the wilderness. Their aim is to inspire the same feelings of love, wonder and awe they themselves have developed for elephants. To anyone with a mind open to impressions of beauty and grandeur, they must surely have succeeded in doing this.

Elephants have a curious effect on human imagination. Throughout the ages people have been fascinated by their size, intelligence and anatomy, and have wanted to get close to or dominate them. Apart from circuses and the isolated experiment in training elephants in the Belgian Congo, the only way to possess an African elephant in the early part of this century was to shoot it. Tusks mounted on the wall and fading photographs of the hunter and his fallen beast serve as a permanent reminder of what was thought of as a glorious encounter with an elephant.

In more recent times, however, a gentler mode of getting close to elephants has been established. We have the astonishing stories of Daphne Sheldrick, who has brought up innumerable baby elephants and given us insight on many similarities in the lives of elephants and man. I was fortunate during the mid-1960s to study elephant behaviour in the wild at Lake Manyara in Tanzania, and found that elephant society was complex, composed of tight-knit family units which often form part of larger 'kinship groups'. The kinship groups themselves might join up to form a 'clan' numbering several hundred individuals. There might be several clans within a population. Cynthia Moss and her colleagues in Amboseli have since charted

One of the world's foremost authorities on the African elephant, Iain Douglas-Hamilton was awarded the O.B.E. in 1992 for his lifelong efforts in elephant conservation. Together with his wife Oria, he is the author of two books, *Among the Elephants* (1975), a detailed record of his five-year study of the elephants of Lake Manyara National Park in Tanzania, and *Battle for the Elephants* (1992), a moving account of the plight of the elephant during the past 20 years. He is the founder of the elephant charity Save the Elephants, and is deeply involved in research into elephant populations across Africa.

the life histories of individual elephants in far greater detail, allowing unprecedented understanding into elephants' social behaviour and their way of life, from the smallest calf to the greatest matriarch and mightiest bull.

The role of the wildlife photographer is a natural complement to this new way of looking at elephants, and Daryl and Sharna Balfour have succeeded in capturing marvellous images of elephant behaviour and the wildlands they live in right across Africa. In their quest to find elephants living in natural, unspoiled environments, they have visited locations that encompass the full range of management practices used by man to deal with elephants in Africa, from the *laissez faire* of Tsavo in Kenya and Chobe in Botswana to the precise and calculated culling of South Africa's Kruger National Park, which has held some 7 500 elephants at a desired density for three decades.

It is a given that those responsible for the future of elephants care passionately for their survival. The means by which this may be achieved, however, are subject to huge differences of outlook and opinion. Because man is still expanding into elephant range, and because arguments for human welfare are politically more powerful than any others, conservation is often forced into a strait-jacket of justifying every conservation action as a service to human needs.

At one end of the spectrum John Hanks believes elephants can only survive by accommodating economic imperatives, even to the extent of trying to open a rationalised ivory trade. Daphne Sheldrick, on the other hand, puts ethical considerations first and is opposed both to the ivory trade and to culling for ecological purposes. Yet these are but two standpoints among elephant aficionados who, whatever their view, have one thing in common – an enormous affection for elephants.

What elephants really think of human beings is another story. They are usually peaceful and tolerant – a huge bull called Baby Huey I once met in Savuti in Botswana allowed me to approach almost within touching distance of him while he shook a camelthorn tree, raining pods on both our heads. His opinion seemed to be that people should simply be ignored. Another elephant, Virgo, my favourite female in Manyara, allowed me to approach within a few feet of her, offering a tantalising promise of man-elephant communication, before the slaughter of this population destroyed the trust we had begun to build. Happily Virgo survived and has become a senior matriarch. The norm, unfortunately, is that most elephants regard people as adversaries.

Daryl's encounter with the huge tusker Tshokwane illustrates the other side of elephant nature, an anti-human behaviour which usually leaves no survivor. Elephants have a remarkably low wounding rate compared to other dangerous game in Africa, such as buffalo, for the simple reason that they are usually very thorough in dealing with adversaries when they come into physical contact. Daryl was lucky.

But consider then the human species from an elephant's point of view. Everything a calf learns from its mother makes it suspicious of people. Every time a scent of humans comes wafting on the breeze she tenses up. Even tame elephants in parks still feel very uneasy if they smell a human being out of their car.

In general elephants are justified in any low opinion in which they might hold the human race. The three major problems elephants face today are all caused by human beings. Firstly, they are facing an expanding human population that invades their range, starts growing crops and then complains when elephants eat this attractive new fodder. Secondly, the displaced elephants are then compressed into the few safe areas set aside for their protection, and start eating woody vegetation faster than it can regenerate. This leads to cries of elephant over-population and calls for them to be culled. Finally, lurking in the background is the ever present danger of the ivory trade, which twice in the last 100 years has spiralled out of hand and threatened to eliminate the vast majority of the elephants in Africa.

This book comes at a time when the barriers have been falling between South Africa and the rest of Africa and where, despite the continent's vast potential resources, there is widespread poverty and land hunger. The allocation of space for wild animals comes under increasing scrutiny as the protected reserves are juxtaposed with rural populations living in impoverished circumstances.

As a result there are tough decisions all down the line. How much space for people, how much for elephants? How many trees are worth the life of an elephant? The decisions cannot be ducked. Those who want elephants at any price have to look at the cost to other plant and animal communities, and to biodiversity.

At the time of writing the whole management of elephants in Kruger National Park, one of the key players in the debate, is under review. A new and daring strategy is being talked about: the idea of experimenting on a giant scale in different parts of Kruger so that the dynamics of elephants, trees, fires, and water supplies can be truly understood. There is hope that elephant density in these experiments can be regulated by translocating whole family units rather than by killing them.

In Kruger National Park, because elephant densities are low, a cessation of culling would probably have little effect on the vegetation in the short term, even if the elephants increase, as they would be expected to do, at five per cent per annum. However, in the long run, unless some form of birth control for elephants is developed, the expected pattern would be for the elephants to increase to the point where they cause major changes in the habitat by the wholesale removal of trees. Therefore, the responsibility for playing God still

*Amboseli provides the ideal open habitat in which to study elephant.*

remains with those in charge of the national parks and reserves. The value of elephants against the value of trees and other creatures that depend on the trees still has to be fully weighed and assessed. As the Balfours have written, 'In the long term it will be the preservation of elephant habitat rather than protection from illegal hunting that will ensure the future of the African elephant.'

In the 1970s, the African elephant population was radically affected by two main factors: an increase in the price of ivory on the world market, itself a consequence of the new buying power of the Japanese and the fashion for using ivory products; and an increase in the availability of automatic weapons in the hands of poachers, a result of the arms race, wars and civil strife. The destructiveness of a single poacher was immensely increased by an automatic rifle and to control poaching was proportionately harder. In these circumstances populations of 'safe' elephants in places like Murchison Falls National Park in Uganda were brought to the edge of extinction within a few years. The people involved in the killing were not just impoverished villagers unable to resist a few dollars for ivory, but more often ruthless gangs of heavily armed bandits, equally willing to rob and rape as to slaughter elephants.

Between 1979 and 1989 I was involved with other scientists in the African Elephant Specialist Group in compiling information on the status of elephant populations across the continent. According to our best estimates the African elephants declined from a minimum estimate of 1,3 million to a maximum estimate of some 609 000. In addition, the mean weight of tusks in the trade declined, indicating that age structures of living elephants had collapsed with the excessive elimination of older elephants carrying heavy ivory. And, in all these years, the elephants were on Appendix II of the CITES treaty, which permitted controlled trade in elephant products and which had little effect in protecting them. Those calling for a reopening of trade in ivory would do well to remember this before arguing that the ivory ban is irrelevant today because it has not worked 100 per cent. The TRAFFIC group (Trade Records Analysis of Flora and Fauna in Commerce) estimated that ivory equivalent to some 700 000 elephants was taken off in that same period. Only parts of southern Africa were an exception to this continental trend, which led to a positive attitude towards continued ivory trade.

In the event the ivory trade ban of 1989 was one of the most successful pieces of conservation legislation of the past few decades and, although it may not have eliminated all ivory poaching and trading, it has been a critical factor in the recovery of elephant populations hard hit by the poaching. It remains the first line of defence against those who kill for ivory. I can personally vouch that, on the aerial surveys I now make in East Africa, there is no comparison with the years of the ivory slaughter. In the 1970s and 1980s I saw fresh elephant carcasses everywhere I flew. Now these are very rare and are only found at the levels which would be expected from natural mortality, or from official killing of elephants in protection of farmers' crops. Indeed in some East African parks and reserves, like Tsavo, the elephants now appear to be on an upward trajectory of recovery. We are convinced in conservation circles in East Africa that a resumption of the ivory trade in any form would lead to a resumption of the uncontrolled illegal trading of the past.

While the ivory trade would not make elephants extinct, I believe it could easily reduce them from thousands to a few hundreds, push some populations to extinction and others through a genetic bottleneck where the survivors would be largely tuskless. This tendency has been seen in the elephants in Addo Elephant National Park in South Africa, which were subjected to intensive selection pressures in the 18th and 19th centuries, and more recently in Queen Elizabeth National Park in Uganda, where, according to Ugandan researcher Eve Abe, heritable tusklessness has increased over the last two decades of intensive ivory poaching. Although greatly reduced, poaching nevertheless still remains a problem, and recent reports have shown that the funding for many African wildlife agencies has fallen. There is no cause for complacency about the effects of the ban, and continued vigilance and support for anti-poaching is vital.

In this context there is a question of what to do with Africa's existing stocks of ivory accruing from animals that die naturally, are shot on crop protection or recovered from poachers. A powerful argument has been made to make money for conservation from limited ivory sales, and to use the proceeds to finance conservation schemes to benefit local people who share the land with elephants. In a country like South Africa, with well-run parks like Kruger, one can imagine such tightly controlled operations working.

Unfortunately, the argument, while compelling, is fatally flawed. All past experience suggests that any legal trade will stimulate a vast, illegal, parallel trade both in Africa and at the consumption end in Asia. Secondly, it is questionable that the proceeds from ivory

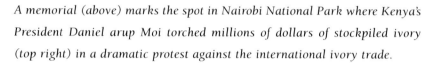

*A memorial (above) marks the spot in Nairobi National Park where Kenya's President Daniel arup Moi torched millions of dollars of stockpiled ivory (top right) in a dramatic protest against the international ivory trade.*

would benefit conservation or the local people, rather than disappearing into the pockets of power brokers. Even in South Africa, where it was once thought things could be carefully controlled, scandals of an illicit ivory trade in the 1980s connected with the military continue to erupt.

Finally, any legal trade would undermine the present climate of disapproval associated with owning ivory, sending out a clear signal that ivory is respectable provided it comes from official sales. Demand for ivory has successfully been killed in the West, although it is still very much alive in the East. Tinkering with limited sales would lend legitimacy to the purchasing of ivory and might well wake up a sleeping giant of demand.

If money is needed for conservation, funds from ivory sales are a red herring. Ivory, even during the recent ivory rush, was never more than a fraction of one per cent of the GNP of any African country. The funds needed for conservation and protection of biodiversity are far greater than could ever be supplied by a limited ivory trade.

It would be much better if it was firmly accepted by all those in authority that the ivory trade should remain shut indefinitely. What would be helpful is a clear statement from conservation leaders like

WWF, TRAFFIC and IUCN that the ivory trade is not an option and should remain closed once and for all. Then African countries can co-operate in finding solutions to poaching and the illegal ivory trade. Trade in skins and meat derived from properly controlled culling done for ecological reasons is another matter and in my opinion can be legitimate and controlled. The culling issue and the ivory trade issue should be kept apart and not be confused.

For the future we need to solve the problem of how people and elephants can live together. I don't pretend to know all the answers. In many parts of Africa humans and elephants are on a collision course competing for space, with the elephant the inevitable loser. Certainly, the parks and reserves need to be defended through good times and bad, and the West should contribute towards some of these expenses. Elsewhere, the economic incentives for local people to benefit from having elephants as neighbours are part of the solution.

In the end, for elephant conservation, as for our own survival, we need to find a way of curbing human population growth and over-exploitation of natural resources on this planet. Elephants provide a challenge to humanity to leave enough space. For if we do it for them we may end up providing breathing space for ourselves too.

There is also an aesthetic ideal that can overreach race, class and economic grouping. It is in this field that the Balfours make their greatest contribution, by sharing their personal vision and their respect for the African elephant's right to share this planet's space.

# FOREWORD BY DR JOHN HANKS

## A SOUTHERN AFRICAN OPINION

In June 1992, the second United Nations Conference on Environment and Development (UNCED) was held in Rio de Janeiro. This highly publicised 'Earth Summit' should have been a point at which there was a genuine shift in global focus and financial commitment towards the environmental problems which the world is facing. At the conference, 178 nations committed themselves to Agenda 21, an ambitious programme to conserve global resources by making sustainable development a reality, not just a slogan. Yet four years after the Earth Summit it seems nothing has changed. The environmental euphoria which greeted Agenda 21 has evaporated. Financial support

Dr John Hanks, a world-renowned conservationist and leading authority on African wildlife, is chief executive for WWF South Africa, a position he has held since 1990. Prior to becoming Professor and Head of the Department of Biological Sciences at the University of Natal, South Africa in 1978, he spent 14 years doing research in various parts of central and southern Africa. During this period he worked in Kafue National Park and the Luangwa Valley in Zambia, research from which formed the basis of his book *The Struggle for Survival: the Elephant Problem* (1979).

agencies who are responsible for managing Africa's national parks and major game reserves? To answer these questions, we need to examine recent events associated with the legal and illegal trade in ivory, and relate this to the trend in elephant population numbers.

Three hundred years ago, elephants were widespread in Africa in all suitable habitats, with the areas constituting present-day South Africa probably supporting at least 100 000 elephants. From 1650 onwards there was a gradual increase in organised human settlement which pushed elephants back as they came into conflict with agriculture. From 1790 there was an enormous growth in the ivory trade with the emergence of professional ivory hunters

to redress the legacies of years of environmental negligence through responsible stewardship has not been forthcoming. Even the principle of sustainable utilisation of natural resources, particularly as it impacts on the people of Africa, has been eroded away by Europeanised protectionist campaigns which are out-of-touch with the harsh socio-economic and environmental realities of Africa.

The controversy surrounding the sale of elephant skins, meat and ivory is a classic example of radically different cultural interpretations of the ethic for living sustainably. Should the elephant be exempt from an evaluation of 'sustainable use' because of ethical considerations? If so, whose ethics? Can the elephant survive in large parts of Africa if it does not have a value other than for viewing by tourists? Will the species ever survive in the protected areas so beautifully illustrated by Daryl and Sharna Balfour, when there have been drastic reductions in the budgets for the law enforcement

and, by 1870, most large elephant populations in South Africa had been destroyed. The killing then spread from southern Africa to West and East Africa in the 19th and early part of the 20th century.

With the collapse in demand for ivory following the First World War and the introduction of wildlife conservation legislation, elephants staged a dramatic recovery. This was not to last, however, with large-scale killing beginning again in 1970 as the demand for ivory increased. Poaching on an unprecedented scale started up in East Africa, spreading from there south and north. A precipitous decline in elephant numbers took place, fuelled by the rapid rise in the demand for ivory in the 1970s and '80s, when the price was driven steadily up from US$60 per kilogram in 1970 to US$300 per kilogram in 1989. The profits to be made were considerable, and Africa's impoverished rural communities found it difficult to resist offers from traders and their middlemen to kill elephants illegally.

With the publication in 1989 of new estimates for African elephant populations showing an alarming decrease in numbers, a world-wide campaign was started to close down the legal trade in ivory. The campaign came to a head at the 7th Conference of the Parties to the Convention of International Trade in Endangered Species of Wild Fauna and Flora (CITES) in Switzerland in October 1989. The southern African states, particularly Zimbabwe and South Africa, wanted the legal, controlled trade to remain in place, arguing that revenue from the sale of elephants and elephant products was going back into both conservation funding and local communities. For example, in South Africa the gross income from the sale of elephant products over the five year period from 1985 to 1989 averaged US$1,4 million per year. These funds accrued directly to the National Parks Board, and helped to offset the costs of security and management of the various reserves under their control, notably Kruger National Park. However, after heated and often acrimonious debate, the majority of delegates voted to ban the legal trade in ivory by moving the elephant from Appendix II of CITES (which permits controlled international commerce in wildlife products) to Appendix I (which prohibits all such trade).

The protagonists of the ivory ban heralded the closure in trade as the start of a new era for elephant conservation. The southern African states remained in firm opposition to the ban, arguing that, with the trade ban in force, there was little incentive to conserve elephants outside protected areas, unless some compensation were to be offered for lost earnings. As such compensation is unlikely to be forthcoming, it makes good sense to give the resource a value and thereby give local communities an incentive to ensure that one of their major sources of income does not disappear.

In June 1991, Botswana, Namibia, Zimbabwe, Zambia and Malawi established the Southern African Centre for Ivory Marketing (SACIM). This was a proposal to control the legal trade through one central marketing point, with the major proportion of the revenue going to an 'elephant conservation fund'. SACIM, however, had little influence on the elephant debate at the 8th Conference of the Parties to CITES in Japan in March 1992, which voted to keep all elephant populations on Appendix I.

At the 9th CITES Conference in November 1994, South Africa submitted a proposal to transfer its elephants from Appendix I to Appendix II to trade internationally in non-ivory products – mainly skins from elephants culled for ecological reasons in Kruger National Park. The funds raised would go back to park management. In the five years prior to the general Appendix I listing coming into place in 1990, Kruger National Park had earned US$340 000 annually from the sale of skins. By 1994, 800 elephant skins were stockpiled in the park. An integral part of South Africa's proposal was the statement that if the proposal was accepted, the country would withdraw its 'reservation' on the Appendix I listing. (Under this reservation, South Africa was exempt from the CITES ivory ban). In other words, South Africa would never again be able to trade in ivory internationally without the approval of CITES.

Those opposed to the South African proposal were concerned that placing South African elephants on Appendix II, even for non-ivory products, would act as a signal for the re-opening of the ivory trade, and would thus stimulate further poaching, although no evidence was brought forward to substantiate this. Opposition to the proposal continued in the build up to the CITES Conference, leaving South Africa with little alternative but to withdraw the proposal at the conference itself.

The focus of the debate for those countries arguing for a lifting or partial lifting of the trade in elephant products is the following question: why should impoverished African countries look after large and potentially destructive animals such as elephants unless they have a value to the country as a whole, or to local communities that are threatened by the presence of elephants? Whether we like it or not, this is one of the most fundamental issues in conservation, and one that we will have to address. The protectionists, mainly from the developed countries, have dominated the last three CITES meetings, and through their interventions, the trade in elephant products has been closed. Is this the right *long-term* approach to ensure that the elephants have a future in Africa? To answer that question, we must consider the economic value of elephants to each country, which can be categorised as follows:

◆  *Direct economic value of elephants*. This includes the sale of ivory, meat, skins, live elephants, safari hunting revenues and tourism. Ivory alone could generate US$50 million per year for African governments. A recent study in East Africa concluded that the 300 000 tourists who visit Kenyan reserves annually bring in US$200 million per year to the local economy, and that the value of viewing elephants in Kenya is in the region of US$25 million per year. This suggests a powerful financial incentive for their non-consumptive use rather than harvesting them for their ivory. However, only a few of the 35 African countries which still have elephant populations have the potential to develop a significant income from the tourism industry, and it is totally unrealistic to extrapolate the Kenyan example to much of the rest of Africa.

◆ *Indirect economic value of elephants.* This is related to the 'ecological role' of elephants, for example by diversifying forests and woodlands, dispersing seeds and opening up waterholes for other species. It is very difficult to quantify these activities in economic terms, and any value derived must be offset against the detrimental cost of elephants associated with their considerable potential to destroy agricultural crops.

◆ *Preservation value.* To NGOs raising funds for wildlife conservation, elephants are prime examples of 'charismatic megaherbivores', attractive and appealing species which have enormous fund-raising pull. In the long-term, these appeals benefit not only elephants, but also their habitats and other species as well. Unfortunately, the efforts of national and international NGOs to prop up ailing wildlife departments in Africa will only be a small drop in the ocean. Tens of millions of dollars are required urgently to put whole departments back on their feet, sums that are way beyond the capacity of private-sector donors.

The sum total of the economic value of elephants to each country is not an easy statistic to quantify, but it should be obtained before rational and objective management decisions can be made about the future of elephants in Africa. On the one side sits Kenya, where elephant stocks are valued much more highly for their tourism-generating capacity than for their ivory. There, an absolute trade ban might be the logical way to go. In contrast, in Zimbabwe, where large sums have been invested in wildlife management programmes involving local communities, such as operation CAMPFIRE, a trade ban will almost certainly result in the loss of hundreds of elephants living outside protected areas because there will no longer be an incentive for their conservation. The ivory trade, if re-opened under the type of *strictly* controlled conditions proposed by SACIM, should not be seen as the death warrant of elephants, but rather as part of a carefully monitored, multi-faceted management programme to conserve Africa's fast-dwindling biological diversity. Whether we happen to like it or not, economic considerations are of paramount importance, because ultimately somebody has to pay the substantial bills for running the traditional protected areas and nature conservation in general. One way to look at these different considerations is to look at what effect the CITES trade ban has had on the illegal killing of elephants and on the ivory trade. To answer this question, representatives of the African Elephant Specialist Group (AESG) and TRAFFIC undertook an extensive examination of the impact of the ivory ban (*see* footnote 1). The study was primarily carried out in nine countries, namely Zimbabwe, Kenya, Tanzania, Cameroon, Malawi, Zambia, Gabon, Ivory Coast and Nigeria. The results of this investigation have far-reaching implications not only for the future management of Africa's elephant, but also for the management of the continent's protected areas. Key points to emerge from the study included the following:

◆ The international ivory trade ban has not halted the illegal killing of elephants. The continued loss of elephants appears to be a result of the inability on the part of range states to protect them.

◆ Law-enforcement budgets in the majority of Africa's protected areas are less than five per cent of the now widely accepted estimate of US$200/km$^2$ required to guarantee the integrity of protected areas and the safety of the 'flagship' species within them.

◆ Throughout the African continent, experienced staff in game parks, reserves and other protected areas are being retrenched and there are significant problems in replacement and recruiting.

◆ The international community, believing that the ivory trade ban would contain the illegal offtake of elephants, have shifted the focus of their funding from the elephant to the rhino crisis, and as a result range state governments have been receiving less external support for activities related to the protection of elephants.

◆ There is little doubt that ivory, in a variety of forms, has continued to be traded both within Africa and internationally since the CITES trade ban took effect, although a number of qualitative indicators do point to some degree of decline. On the other hand, seizures of illegal ivory are increasing in Zambia, and there is evidence of Asian-run ivory processing operations taking root in a number of countries in Africa.

◆ The nine countries surveyed have nearly 100 tonnes of ivory stockpiled between them, with Tanzania and Zimbabwe holding the greatest volume. Kenya and Zambia have burned ivory in the past, but whether this policy will be continued remains unclear.

*The reduction of riverine forest along the banks of the Chobe in Botswana is mainly a result of increased pressure from elephant herds. The dilemma is whether to allow environmental modification or control numbers by culling.*

Reports of human-elephant conflict have increased in the majority of African elephant range states since the institution of the ban, resulting in many more elephants being killed either by government authorities or local communities in self-defence. On the basis of human population growth patterns and the subsequent reduction in available wilderness areas, the population of the African elephant will continue to decline even if illegal killing for the commercial trade in ivory is brought under control.

The message to come from the AESG/TRAFFIC study is there for all the world to see, and it is this. If African countries opt for a strong 'protectionist' policy towards wildlife and exclude the possibility of consumptive use, the cost will overwhelm them. If conservationists continue to regard a legal ivory trade as an anathema, they will be turning a blind eye to the realities of Africa. The

key to the future of elephants lies with good management, whatever route is chosen for their conservation. Consumptive use programmes (including the ivory trade) will also fail without good management, particularly when people are poor, and basic internal infrastructure has broken down.

Africa's wildlife heritage as a whole, let alone elephants, will not survive unless the problems of serious underfunding addressed in the AESG/TRAFFIC report receives urgent attention, and only a massive intervention by bilateral and multilateral aid agencies can rectify the situation. Surely the will must be there after the Earth Summit? The challenge for those southern African states who are protagonists of the ivory trade and of using wildlife sustainably is to convince the rest of the world that a policy of utilisation is a perfectly acceptable form of conservation, and one which does *not* turn against all ethical and aesthetic considerations, both of which remain powerful motivating forces for conserving the African elephant.

1. Dublin, HT, Milliken T & Barnes, RFW. (1994) *Four years after the CITES ban: illegal killing of elephants, ivory trade and stockpiles.* A report of the IUCN/SSC Elephant Specialist Group.

# FOREWORD BY DAPHNE SHELDRICK

## THE MORAL VIEWPOINT

I t is an honour to have been invited to write a foreword to Daryl and Sharna Balfour's breathtaking book, celebrating the majestic African elephant; one in which the authors' sensitivity and respect for these gentle giants is mirrored in their photographic genius.

It is also a privilege to have been equipped by destiny to speak for the elephants, for my life has been intertwined with that of these magnificent and awe-inspiring animals for more than 40 years. Thirty of these have been spent living among them in Kenya's Tsavo National Park where my late husband and I shared in their joys and sorrows and spent endless enchanted hours watching and studying them as they went about

As the wife of David Sheldrick, park warden in Tsavo East National Park in Kenya in the 1960s and '70s, Daphne hand-reared orphaned baby elephants found in the park with the aim of re-introducing them into the wild. In doing so, she has developed a remarkable understanding of elephants and established relationships with them which have lasted for decades. For her efforts she was recently awarded the MBE. Daphne is the author of *The Orphans of Tsavo* (1966) and *The Tsavo Story* (1973).

calamities. All have come to us bereft and traumatised, and their grieving for lost loved ones has been heartbreaking to behold. Those newborn infant elephants that we have managed to save today range in age from eight months to nine years. All will live as wild elephants again among their own kind, as have many others that were orphaned over the milk-dependent age of two years and who joined the wild herds at puberty. Today one of these is a matriarch in her own right aged 37 who, despite the suffering inflicted on her kind through poaching, still displays a loyal fondness for the humans that saved her life. I have always tried to analyse animal behaviour

their lives. We experienced the dark decades of poaching which devastated their numbers and disrupted their society, their suffering which was so intense it was almost tangible and terrible beyond words. We came to understand the complexity of their recycling role within the environment; that what at first might appear as wasteful and wanton destruction is, in fact, a subtle process of renewal and change ordained by Nature. We also witnessed the mass natural die-off of elephants during drought and food shortages once their role had been completed, which gave rise to the long-held myth of the elephants' graveyard, and, although this too was terrible to see, we knew instinctively that Nature's way provided a more humane and lasting solution to the restless oscillation of the differing species, for, as surely as the sun and moon move across the skies, nothing in Nature remains static.

The past 10 years of my life have been devoted to hand-rearing the young of elephants. Most of these were orphaned by mankind's insatiable greed for ivory, although some were as a result of natural

through lay eyes, ignoring the out-moded thinking that precludes a human interpretation of animal behaviour, irrespective of how 'human' that behaviour might be. As a naturalist I have come to view things differently, knowing that Nature relies on a basic blueprint to characterise the different forms of life on earth, and that many of the traits inherent in the human animal have been duplicated in others, and especially in the elephants.

Elephants and humans have many things in common: a similar lifespan, for instance, and a parallel rate of development. In the same way as humans, elephants have a strong sense of family, and a sense of death. They 'bury' their dead, covering a body with sticks and leaves, and return periodically to pay their respects. They pine and mourn just as we do and, of course, they remember, for the memory of an elephant surpasses even that of man. They can also display their deep feelings of compassion and sometimes this will even extend to other creatures in distress.

Like Daryl Balfour, I too once found myself lying with a broken leg at the mercy of an elephant, spared when I could so easily have been killed. There was compassion in the eyes of the elephant as it stood towering over me, contemplating its next move; eventually it turned and slowly walked away. I was humbled by this in view of what little compassion has been extended to the elephants by humans.

Elephants have also been endowed with many of the attributes we humans lack: telepathic powers of communication, the ability to reach across the miles through infrasound below human hearing range and that mystical genetic memory we term 'instinct'. However, like ourselves, they also have to learn, and the wisdom of the elders is passed from one generation to the next.

Through my long and intimate association with elephants I have also come to understand some of the workings of the elephant mind, and this has been a very illuminating and salutary lesson. Their brain is convoluted very like our own, which suggests that they reason and think. I also know that emotionally elephants are similar to humans. In childhood they display all the traits of human children – they can

*Tsavo, location of Daphne Sheldrick's work with orphaned baby elephants.*

be happy, lonely or sad, mischievous, contrary, competitive, stubborn or moody, and they can be delightful, co-operative and endearing beyond words. They 'feel' as we do, and this truth must surely raise some disturbing questions about the way elephants are handled in some African countries. For instance, it would be out of bounds for a human child to be sold into bondage for gain, its family first having been butchered before its very eyes. It would be cruel and inhumane to dump young human children in unknown territory, leaving them to get on with their own lives as best they can without the guidance and security of adults. Yet both are common practice in elephant management – as though psychological ethics is something many wildlife authorities find more convenient to ignore, sheltering behind the shield of 'good science'.

Fortunately this is something that is increasingly being called to account as the nature of elephants becomes more generally known and understood. Elephants should be handled with sensitivity and compassion, not with brutality and callousness. They should be handled as humanely as possible, for they are indeed very 'human' animals, richly endowed with all the better attributes of mankind, and very few of the bad.

# ABOUT ELEPHANTS

## MAGNIFICENT ELEPHANTS

The massive African savannah elephant is undoubtedly the most spectacular land animal – powerful, dignified and imposing, lord of all it surveys. And a big tusker is surely the most magnificent sight in the animal kingdom. His huge ears spread wide, head raised inquiringly, thick, creamy tusks protruding like scythes from his upper jaw, he can stand up to four metres tall and weigh six or seven tonnes. His tusks, or ivory, can extend to three metres each and weigh as much as 100 kilograms, the heaviest recorded tipping the scales at 102,7 kilograms. These came from the slopes of Mount Kilimanjaro and are locked away in a vault in the British Museum Perhaps the most famous elephant of them all, the legendary Ahmed who roamed the hills and valleys of Kenya's Marsabit National Park until he died in 1974, carried ivory that topped 67 kilograms on each side, while most of the once

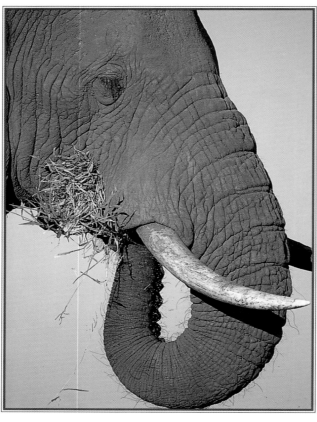

*ABOVE: Elephants enjoy a wide variety of fodder, ranging from thorny acacia to tender shoot and lush new grass.*
*OPPOSITE: An Okavango bull, lord of the savannah.*
*PREVIOUS PAGE: A group of bulls share a Savuti waterhole with a lone kudu and several impala.*

with younger bulls carrying smaller, less unwieldy ivory. Tshokwane, the huge Kruger Park bull that trampled and seriously injured me in 1992, was unable to deliver the coup de grâce because his tusks were too long for him to get down on his knees to crush me with the base of his trunk and forehead, as elephants usually do with their victims. Shortly after this incident Tshokwane broke one of his massive tusks. Could this have been to rid himself of an awkward encumbrance? Apart from fighting, sparring and jousting, an elephant uses its tusks almost continuously while feeding, using them in conjunction with its trunk in breaking branches, peeling bark, stripping off thorns or foliage and digging for roots, bulbs, tubers and water. Like man, elephants are usually left or right 'handed' and will use one tusk almost exclusively. This commonly results in the tusk in use becoming ridged or grooved where vegetation is regularly pulled across it, worn down or even broken off short.

renowned 'Magnificent Seven' big tuskers in South Africa's Kruger National Park, along with several of the park's more recent residents, were in the 60 kilogram-plus category. The right tusk of Phelwana, one of Kruger's legendary tuskers, tipped 71,7 kilograms.

An elephant's tusks are in fact its only two front teeth, or incisors, which continue to grow throughout life. Unlike the molars, which are worn down and replaced up to six times during a lifetime, tusks never grow again if they are lost. Males carry longer, thicker and hence heavier tusks than females, which can reach such a length that they touch the ground when the animal stands at rest. Such long tusks are undoubtedly a hindrance, and there are a number of instances of big tuskers being badly gored and even killed in fights

Tusk length and condition also depends to a large extent upon the quality of the elephants' foodstuff, and where various mineral deficiencies occur this manifests itself in the size and shape of the ivory. The elephants of Etosha generally have stunted, broken tusks of very brittle ivory due to such a deficiency – a characteristic that has made this population of little interest to ivory poachers.

Because of the influence of the elephant's diet on its ivory, it is now possible to identify the area of origin of ivory by isotopic analysis, ultimately leading to the possibility that a database similar to the American FBI's 'fingerprint file' could be established, allowing immediate identification of the origins of poached ivory. Such information could be used to track down poaching and smuggling syndicates.

Additionally, the origins of 'legal' ivory, such as that obtained by park managers from culled animals or those dying a natural death, could be accurately certified, which could help in shutting down the black market should ivory trading ever be legalised again.

# ORIGINS

The hyrax is a smallish, furry inhabitant of rugged mountains, rocky crevices and leafy tree-tops. The manatee, on the other hand, is a sluggish, ungainly sea creature. Unlikely as it may seem, these are the elephant's closest living relatives, a relationship confirmed by physiological and biochemical evidence, and evolutionary ancestors.

Little is known about the origins of the unique mammalian order Proboscidea (animals with trunks), the family most closely linked with Sirenia (manatees and dugongs) and Hyracoidea (hyraxes, or conies). The earliest-known member of the Proboscidea order are pig-sized herbivores called Moeritheres, which lived in north Africa between 55 and 40 million years ago. Another branch of the family tree, the Palaeomastodons, existed 40–25 million years ago and, with their short trunks, began to take on more of the shape we recognise in elephants today. It was only in the Miocene Era, however, some 25–5 million years ago, that creatures with large bodies, big ears and long trunks and tusks appeared. Among these were the Primelephas,

Gomphotherium and Deinotherium, with other branches of the family, such as the Mammut, Mammuthus (mammoth) and Stegodon, still alive as recently as 10 000 years ago. Fossil remains indicate that the Mammut, or mastodon, which lived in North America, reached an evolutionary dead end and became extinct towards the end of the last Ice Age 12 000 to 10 000 years ago and is therefore not a predecessor of the modern elephant. The Stegodon evolved in Asia at the same time as true elephants were appearing in Africa, but later died out. Primelephas was the antecedent of the three most recent forms of the Elephantoidea: African elephant, *Loxodonta africana*, Asian elephant, *Elephas maximus*, and woolly mammoth, *Mammuthus primigenius*. It is evident from the evolutionary tree that the mammoth was more closely related to the Asian than the African elephant, although both the latter species originated in Africa. The African elephant, however, evolved solely in Africa and, while it migrated across the continent, it did not leave it; fossil remains show that the Asian elephant originated in Africa but migrated to Asia and parts of Europe.

While the mammoth died out as recently as 5 000 years ago – recent Russian investigations maintain that their demise was partly as a result of hunting by early man, and partly because of global warming as the Ice Age came to an end – the Asian and African elephants thrived, branching into the separate sub-species we know today.

*The elephant's foot is constructed in such a way that the animal is virtually walking on tip-toe, with a tough, fatty pad of connective tissue for the sole.*

*An elephant's eye is small in relation to its head and it has correspondingly poor eyesight, particularly at distances of more than 50–100 metres.*

| | AFRICAN ELEPHANT | | ASIAN ELEPHANT | | |
|---|---|---|---|---|---|
| | **Savannah** Loxodonta africana africana | **Forest** Loxodonta africana cyclotis | **Sri Lankan** Elephas maximus maximus | **Mainland** Elephas maximus indicus | **Sumatran** Elephas maximus sumatranus |
| **Height** | 3–4 metres | 2–3 metres | 2–3,5 metres | 2–3 metres | 2–2,5 metres |
| **Weight** | 4–7 tonnes | 2–4 tonnes | 3–5 tonnes | 2,5–4,5 tonnes | 2–4 tonnes |
| **Colour** | grey | dark grey | grey with large areas of depigmentation | lighter grey | very light grey |

## PHYSIOLOGY

Elephants are the largest land mammals, second only to the great whales as the largest living creatures. Three sub-species of Asian and two of African elephants are recognised, but, while numbers of Asian elephants appear to be stable or increasing in numbers, the African is in a serious decline, slaughtered for their ivory from which jewellery and decorative ornaments are fabricated. The Asian and African elephants are in fact so different from each other that they are classified in separate genera. The Asian elephant is much smaller than its African cousin, both in height and mass, with tiny ears by comparison. Only bull Asian elephants carry tusks, and even then 40–50 per cent are tuskless. An Asian elephant's tusks are usually short and thin, occasionally long and slender, and it is unusual for them to attain any great thickness or weight. Unlike the African elephant, which has two 'fingers' at the tip of its trunk, the Asian elephant has but one. The Asian elephant's forehead is prominently domed and its

*Sexing elephants from the rear is difficult as the bull's testes are located inside the body, and the female genitalia are situated between the hind legs.*

*Elephant tusks are overgrown incisors protruding from the upper jaw. They consist mostly of dentine and grow at a rate of 15–18 centimetres per year.*

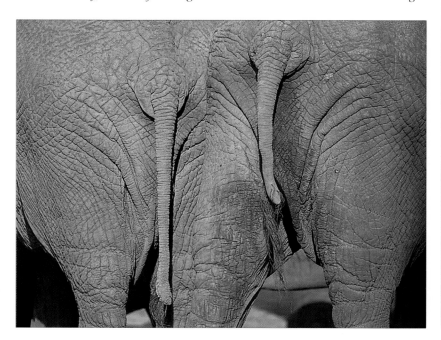

*When the first white settlers arrived in Africa, the spoils of the continent were its slaves, gold and ivory. Tens of thousands of elephants were slaughtered by professional hunters to satisfy the demand for trinkets, piano keys and billiard balls carved from their tusks.*

back arched, hump-like. The molars of the Asian elephant have parallel ridges and a rasp-like surface, while those of the African elephant are lozenge-shaped (hence Loxodonta). Asian elephants frequently exhibit whitish or pink patches of depigmentation.

Domesticated Asian elephants are widely used for forest clearing, logging and ceremonial events, and, while it was long believed that African elephants could not be 'tamed', they have been used in parts of Africa in agricultural activities and elephant-back safaris.

*Loxodonta africana cyclotis*, the African forest elephant, is also smaller than its savannah relative, with smaller ears and long, slender tusks, often straight or even down-curved. Shy and secretive, they possibly number more than official counts reveal, though poaching in central and west Africa has decimated their numbers.

## IN PURSUIT OF WHITE GOLD

Elephants range throughout sub-Saharan Africa in virtually all ecotypes, from open savannah to dense equatorial rainforests, high mountains to seashore, and arid desert to lush swamp. Only in relatively recent times has this range become fragmented due to conflict with human populations. The resultant habitat loss has been a major cause of declining elephant numbers. Records show that elephants once roamed Africa from the shores of the Mediterranean in the north to the slopes of Table Mountain in the south. The Roman historian Pliny noted in AD 77 that due to ivory hunting large elephant tusks could no longer be found 'in our part of the world' – referring to the Mediterranean basin – and by the end of the Roman Empire elephants were extinct in North Africa. The Dutch East India Company hoped for big profits from trading in ivory when it settled the Cape in 1652, and Jan van Riebeeck and other early settlers recorded in 1654 that 'within a day's tramp of Cape Town there were elephants, rhinoceros, bloubok and hippo ...' Van Riebeeck's first mention of ivory in his journal is a record of three tusks bartered from Hottentot hunters for 250 grams of tobacco! The arrival of more settlers in the Cape, along with more modern methods of hunting, soon led to the decimation of the area's wildlife, and soon it became necessary for big game hunters to venture further and further north. It was not until 1822, however, that the British governor in the Cape, Lord Charles Somerset, proclaimed elephants 'Royal Game,' meaning they could be hunted only with a special permit from the Governor's office. In 1892 President Paul Kruger of the South African Republic amended laws existing at the time to prohibit the hunting of elephants, as well as rhinos, setting licence fees, instituting a closed season and, at the same time, barring hunters from all State lands. With increasing protection and management, South Africa's elephant population recovered from a low of 120 animals in 1920 to more than 10 000 in 1996.

Since those early attempts at legislating against the slaughter of elephants, primarily for their ivory, similar laws have been promulgated in almost every African state that has or had elephant populations. These proved very successful for the first part of the 20th century, until a disturbing downward spiral began again in the 1970s. Following proposals from Tanzania and Kenya, in October 1989 in Lausanne, Switzerland, the 7th Meeting of the Conference of Parties to the Convention on International Trade in Endangered Species of Wild Fauna and Flora (CITES) voted the African elephant on toits Appendix I – animals threatened with extinction – and hence banned all international trade in ivory (and all other elephant products) outright. Subsequent moves to have the elephant downlisted to Appendix II, primarily by southern African states with healthy elephant populations, have gained little support.

## THE STATE OF THE DEBATE

The attempts by some countries to legalise the ivory trade revolve around the widely accepted conservation policy of sustainable utilisation of wildlife resources; certain countries, specifically South Africa and Zimbabwe and, to a lesser extent, Malawi, maintain their conservation and wildlife management policies have been so effective that elephant numbers need to be strictly controlled and regulated – culled – to ensure that they do not dominate and destroy their own environment to the detriment of other animals, including themselves. These countries believe that they should be able to profit from the fruits of their good management, selling ivory and other elephant by-products resulting from such cropping and raising revenue from trophy hunting, then ploughing this revenue back into conservation.

There are, however, problems associated with such policies. In many African states revenue earned from wildlife utilisation goes directly into central government coffers, with only a fraction, if any, finding its way back into conservation. And elephants are not, perhaps, the ready resource some countries believe them to be. Of the southern African countries who have in the past supported the trade in elephant products, Botswana and Namibia – at the time of writing – have no culling operations (although Botswana intends allowing a limited amount of trophy hunting from 1996 on), Malawi has a relatively small, stable population, Zambia's elephants have been decimated by poaching and those in Mozambique and Angola were almost annihilated in lengthy civil wars during which ivory was used to finance arms purchases and elephant meat to feed hungry troops and starving populations. Zimbabwe has suffered a huge increase in ivory poaching since its rhino population was almost wiped out by poachers, and infighting among the country's politicians and wildlife establishment has sadly damaged its international credibility considerably, to the extent that previously accepted data and population estimates are now being questioned.

South Africa, to date, has experienced minimal poaching, though this can be expected to escalate, particularly if the ivory trade should ever be re-opened. South Africa's initial position at the 1994 CITES meeting was to remove its formal objection to the ivory trade ban in return for a downlisting that would allow them to trade in elephant meat, hides and hair, as well as live animals. However, South Africa's delegates withdrew their proposal at the eleventh hour after experiencing the depth and vehemence of opinion against them. It should be noted that the CITES ban does not restrict domestic trade, and ivory and elephant hide and hair curios (and elephant-meat pies and biltong) have been widely sold in the Kruger National Park as well as in curio shops throughout South Africa.

Also detracting from the credibility of the states pushing for a downlisting at the 1994 CITES meeting was the presence among them of Sudan – a country whose military was seen to be heavily involved in elephant poaching not so long ago – who wanted to be allowed to market its stockpile of 'legal' ivory! Their application was firmly rejected.

It is worth bearing in mind that in 1977 the African elephant was put on CITES Appendix II specifically as a means of controlling the illegal ivory trade and drying up the black market in poached tusks. That this measure was an abject failure is now recorded history – CITES and related bodies proved to be incapable of regulating the legal trade – and there can be no guarantees that such a measure

*Poached for its ivory, an elephant carcass lies near the banks of the Chobe, evidence of cross border raids from nearby Zambia or Namibia.*

could or would succeed today. There are just too many profits to be made on the illegal black market – by the poachers, the traders, the middlemen and the corrupt officials who in the past found it so easy to issue false documentation certifying the legality of poached ivory. South African investigative journalist De Wet Potgieter warns, in his fascinating and controversial book *Contraband: South Africa and the International Trade in Ivory and Rhino Horn* (Quellerie, 1995), that South Africa was in fact one of the worst wildlife 'outlaws' in the world and that its good conservation record was 'one of the apartheid regime's biggest lies'. He warns those supporting calls for a resumption of ivory marketing that the illegal trade in ivory (and rhino horn) is a dangerous, well established, lucrative and cutthroat business in South Africa, supported to a large degree by corrupt officialdom.

International trading in ivory remains illegal, and any move to re-establish the trade once again will certainly open loopholes for the laundering of illegal ivory on to the world market, just as has happened in the past. In the words of Daphne Sheldrick, 'Every piece of ivory is a haunting reminder of a once proud and majestic being.' The use of ivory for any purpose whatsoever should quite simply be regarded as abhorrent and socially unacceptable.

## THE CULLING FIELDS

Culling, the term used for the selective killing of ostensibly surplus animals, has controversial connotations, not the least because of the disputes among biologists and ecologists over the justification, necessity, scientific basis or ethics of killing. At the one end of the scale, Kenya and Botswana follow a policy of minimum intervention in their parks, preferring to allow a natural order to develop. At the opposite end of the spectrum South Africa and Zimbabwe have a hands-on policy, managing and manipulating constantly. The former policy can only work in large (unfenced) areas, the latter is a virtual necessity in smaller (fenced) parks or game reserves.

South Africa's Kruger National Park, one of the largest in Africa, has been culling elephants since 1968, maintaining a population of around 7 000–7 500. Many believe this is too low, as bush encroachment, something that could be prevented by a larger elephant population, is one of the biggest obstacles to full enjoyment of large sectors of the park by visitors. With between 400 and 500 elephants being culled every year, some 10 000–15 000 elephants have been killed since the policy was introduced.

However, with the removal of much of the fencing along the western borders of Kruger National Park, and proposals to create an international 'megapark' extending east into Mozambique and north into Zimbabwe, South Africa's major tourist attraction could hopefully soon be able to stop the culling and accommodate a far greater number of elephants than at present . . . particularly if one of the incentives for culling – profit from ivory, skin and meat – remains closed. When we compare South Africa's total elephant population of 10 000 with Zimbabwe's 68 000, Botswana's 70 000–75 000, Zambia's 22 000–26 000, Tanzania's 86 000 and Kenya's 19 000, there seems to be latitude for a large increase in elephant numbers in South Africa. Kenya's Tsavo East and West national parks combined are similar in size, habitat and rainfall to Kruger, yet before the drought of 1970–1974 the park and its immediate surrounds maintained a population of approximately 45 000 elephants. In the mid-1960s, shortly before the drought, wildlife scientists decided to cull in Tsavo, but strong public opposition – as well as that of the then park warden David Sheldrick – was such that the scheme was abandoned. Subsequent events showed that the culling decision might well have proven disastrous, as about 9 000 Tsavo elephants died during the drought years, while the poaching epidemic which started in the early 1970s, and continued unabated until the banning of the ivory trade in 1989, accounted for about 30 000 more! Tsavo's elephant population, decimated by these dual effects, dropped to less than 7 000 during these years.

Happily though, Tsavo's numbers are once again escalating and in June 1994, during an aerial census of the park's elephants, we saw a single herd numbering at least 800, along with a number of other herds ranging in size from 100 to 400.

Another major objection to culling operations, particularly those carried out on a regular, annual basis, is the way in which it can affect the entire elephant population of a park. Elephants, research has shown, are capable of communicating with one another over distances up to 15 kilometres with infrasonic sounds and rumbles. There can be no doubt that, when culling begins, the distress of the animals is communicated over great distances to other elephant herds, spreading fear and panic. Several years ago, at a private lodge outside Hwange National Park in Zimbabwe, a group of visitors were watching a herd of elephants peacefully drinking and bathing at a waterhole. Suddenly, without any sign of disturbance, the elephants

flew into a panic and fled the scene. Rangers later tracked the elephants to the furthest corner of the reserve, and subsequently discovered that almost to the minute of the perceived panic, elephant culling had started in a sector of the national park almost 80 kilometres away. One theory was that the distress of the slaughter was transmitted either by the elephants involved in the cull over that great distance, or passed from herd to herd through the area, so that all elephants knew within minutes of the slaying of their kind!

Comparison of the behaviour of elephant herds such as those in Amboseli National Park, Kenya, where culling has never been carried out, with that of elephants in parks where culling is a regular occurrence, shows marked differences. Amboseli, Chobe and Etosha elephants show little fear of man or vehicles, and excellent viewing of breeding herds with young are typical daily occurrences. Where elephants are culled regularly or harassed by poachers, the breeding herds tend to hide away, becoming almost entirely nocturnal in their visits to a waterhole, river's edge or lakeside.

A recent development in this contentious issue was that, following a public debate held in Gauteng, South Africa, in May 1995, at which strong opposition to the practice of culling was expressed, the National Parks Board of South Africa announced that it would undertake an in-depth review of the elephant management policies in Kruger National Park. The initial findings of this review were discussed at a meeting of the African Elephant Specialist Group at the

*Carcasses of a culled elephant herd awaiting transportation to the Kruger National Park's meat-processing plant at Skukuza.*

park's headquarters in Skukuza in February 1996. Leading from the recommendations of the AESG, it was announced that a revised elephant management policy for Kruger would be formulated and that the annual elephant cull would not take place in 1996. For the first time in 29 years, no breeding herd elephants would be killed in Kruger and consequently no juvenile elephants would be available for sale. However, family groups would continue to be translocated whenever suitable destinations were available. These moves should be applauded, for they represent a step in the right direction, closer towards mainstream opinions with regard to elephant conservation.

At the same meeting, the National Parks Board also addressed the controversial issue of pressing for a downlisting of elephant products from CITES Appendix I to Appendix II. However, it was decided that the time was not right as any support for downlisting had to be seen in the light of the severe criticism of South African authorities by TRAFFIC, the international animal trade monitoring group, regarding the country's inability to control the trade in wildlife products, notably ivory and rhino horn.

The board did, however, reaffirm its support for elephant culling as a valid management option and indicated that it would continue to support downlisting initiatives once certain basic conditions were met. These included satisfying TRAFFIC that the trade in wildlife products could be properly controlled through appropriate and enforceable legislation.

## THE BABY TRADE

While the concept of culling remains anathema to many, recent successes in the relocation of entire herds of elephants, pioneered by the Zimbabwe wildlife authorities and taken further by South Africa's National Parks Board during the 1994 cull, present a more acceptable alternative for the future. In the past, elephant relocations have involved sparing only elephant calves between the age of one and six years old from the culls, then moving these orphans to holding pens or, occasionally, directly to their new homes. There has been considerable criticism of this practice, with some elephant behaviourists maintaining that it is a recipe for the creation of delinquent herds, and others decrying the blatant immorality of the act.

Baby elephants must learn nearly every life skill from adult elephants, just as a human child does, and their world is dominated by familial social structures. The mother, aunts and elder brothers and sisters all play an important role in raising and educating a young elephant, and, while males will leave the family unit when they reach puberty (at between 10 and 15 years of age), females will usually spend their whole life in the security of a closely knit, co-ordinated clan of family members. It stands to reason that orphans deprived of the security of growing up among their families and the education concomitant thereto are likely to develop severe 'emotional' disorders and have the potential to become violent, aggressive and anti-social.

In the early years of the newly created Pilanesberg National Park in South Africa, cull orphans from Kruger National Park were introduced to the park. Several of these died while still in the holding pens, while after their release some refused to depart the vicinity of their pens and wandered aimlessly.

It was only some time later, when two adult elephant cows were brought from the United States by elephant handler Randall Moore and returned to the wild, that these young elephants showed signs of settling down into proper herd life, with the cows, Durga and Owalla, readily adapting to their new roles as surrogate matriarchs. Recent attacks on several other wild animals in this park, particularly the rhinos, by 'delinquent' elephants have been put down to the

*OPPOSITE: In the wild, youngsters benefit from close family relationships.*
*BELOW: Orphaned calves in pens awaiting translocation from Kruger National Park to other game parks and zoos. Such elephants, deprived of a normal upbringing within the family circle, may become delinquents in time.*

possibility that they may be 'psychologically disturbed' as a result of the very traumatic experiences suffered by them earlier in their lives. Similarly, the adoption of juveniles returned to Tsavo National Park from Daphne Sheldrick's elephant orphanage outside Nairobi by the matriarch Eleanor, herself once a hand-reared orphan, has ensured a far easier re-adaptation to life in the wild

Another possible alternative to the culling of elephants could be the temporary sterilisation of bull elephants by a contraceptive 'pill' or implant. South African scientist Professor Gerard van der Horst of the Physiology Department at the University of the Western Cape maintains it would be possible to 'induce temporary sterility in males by stopping sperm production', which he says would create the least disturbance of all current methods of elephant population control. While methods of female contraception are more advanced than for males, he maintains it is possible and would disturb fewer animals if only dominant bulls were 'sterilised'.

## DESTRUCTION OR DEVELOPMENT?

So long as mankind imposes its own theories on how best to govern nature, there will be conflicts of opinion. It seems ironic that when elephants do what they appear to have evolved to do – push over and uproot trees – it is termed 'destruction', yet when man does the same thing he does so in the name of 'development'. It has been estimated that mankind is clearing more forests per day than all the elephants in Africa 'destroy' in a year. Stephen Gichangi, warden of Tsavo East National Park, expressed his dismay when we visited him on the eve of the 1994 cull in Kruger National Park. 'Here we are in Kenya, prepared to shoot people who kill elephants,' he said, 'yet the South Africans can go out in helicopters and massacre whole herds because they worry they may push down too many trees. It's crazy . . . elephants were made by nature to do that.'

Elephants are intertwined with natural vegetation cycles and, when an elephant pushes down a tree, it in fact destroys very little and simply modifies the landscape. As much as 80 per cent of what is consumed by the elephant is returned, barely digested, to the soil in the form of highly fertile manure, while the remainder of the tree is fed upon by other creatures or decomposes, regenerating as new growth or enriching the earth for other vegetation. As was experienced in Tsavo, woodland is opened up and modified into savannah grassland for a long period but, with changing climatic conditions and long, regular rainy

seasons, the process can easily be reversed. Park managers should be wary of taking too short-term a view of such natural cycles. More importantly, a distinct line must be drawn between the need to cull elephants to maintain an optimum carrying capacity and the need to crop annually to satisfy economic requirements. There is the danger that the budgetary economics of maintaining a modern meat-processing plant like that near Skukuza in Kruger National Park, with the annual realities of covering staff wages and other overheads, could cloud issues to the extent that the tail ends up wagging the dog. Culling, if justified, should be done on the basis of what is best for the ecosystem (and least disturbing to the elephants), and only after long and careful consideration of every factor affecting populations.

As wildlife film-maker and long-time Tsavo ranger and resident Simon Trevor comments in his 1990 film *The Elephants of Tsavo: Love and Betrayal*, 'Elephants will continue to be betrayed (for their ivory) so long as the demand is there. Unless everyone sees ivory as socially repulsive and therefore worthless, the killing will go on.'

There are, and there will continue to be, many debates surrounding this subject. The intensity of debate is surely testimony to the value and importance of elephants to all of us. However, in the long term it will be the preservation of elephant habitat rather than protection from illegal hunting that will ensure the future of the African elephant. Man must be prepared to find workable solutions not only in the way it chooses to deal with elephants, but in the way it manages itself.

*Elephants do not senselessly destroy their environment, but rather modify it by opening up dense woodlands and allowing grasslands to regenerate.*

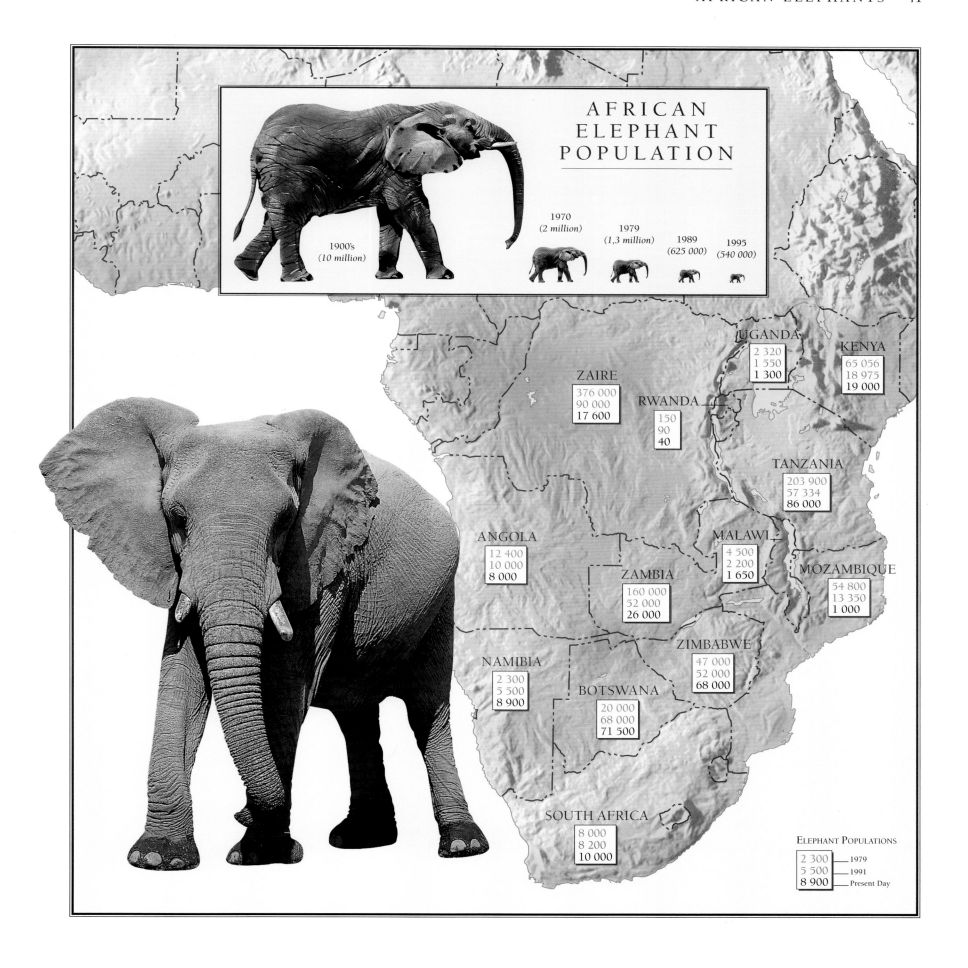

# AFRICAN ELEPHANT POPULATION

1900's
(10 million)

1970
(2 million)

1979
(1,3 million)

1989
(625 000)

1995
(540 000)

UGANDA
2 320
1 550
1 300

KENYA
65 056
18 975
19 000

ZAIRE
376 000
90 000
17 600

RWANDA
150
90
40

TANZANIA
203 900
57 334
86 000

ANGOLA
12 400
10 000
8 000

MALAWI
4 500
2 200
1 650

MOZAMBIQUE
54 800
13 350
1 000

ZAMBIA
160 000
52 000
26 000

ZIMBABWE
47 000
52 000
68 000

NAMIBIA
2 300
5 500
8 900

BOTSWANA
20 000
68 000
71 500

SOUTH AFRICA
8 000
8 200
10 000

ELEPHANT POPULATIONS
2 300 — 1979
5 500 — 1991
8 900 — Present Day

# SAMBURU
# NATIONAL RESERVE

By the meandering, muddy waters of the sluggish Uaso Nyiro River and the rocky, steep-sided crags of Koitogor and Lolkoitoi, Samburu National Reserve, together with its neighbouring parks Buffalo Springs and Shaba, offers a window into the wild beauty of Kenya's rugged Northern Frontier District, where rainfall is sparse. Tiny in comparison by most African standards, the 225-square kilometre reserve, which attracts up to 700 elephants from the surrounding wilderness in the dry season, is one of Kenya's essential safari destinations.

Towering doum palms (*Hyphaene coriacea*) (*right*), with their long, statuesque trunks, dominate the riverine vegetation, while the ubiquitous umbrella tree (*Acacia tortilis*) offers welcome visual relief amid the jumbled landscape of rocky volcanic inselbergs and dry, coarsely scoured riverbeds. While the area is prone to lengthy and sustained droughts, the Uaso Nyiro courses like a lifeline along Samburu's western boundary. Like Angola's Cubango (Kavango) River which flows into Botswana's Okavango Delta, the Uaso Nyiro does not reach the sea, emptying instead into the Lorian swamps on the fringe of the remote Sabena desert. In the past, these swamps provided a valuable dry-season refuge for many thousands of elephants before raiding poachers from nearby Somalia wiped them out.

Samburu is home to a startling array of wildlife which has adapted to life under harsh, semi-desert conditions. Though dominated by its roving elephant herds, here we also found scores of the beautiful and increasingly rare Grevy's zebra and beisa oryx, both Kirk's and Guenther's dik-diks, the olive baboon (*right*), the odd-looking gerenuk and the spectacularly marked reticulated giraffe. Elephants frequent the mature woodlands along the Uaso Nyiro, browsing the lush riverine growth, drinking from its muddy waters, playing in the shade of majestic acacias or simply frolicking in its refreshing shallows.

Jousting and sparring between young male elephants is just one aspect of their preparation for adulthood, when they will compete with rival bulls for the rights to a female in oestrus, or exert their dominance to attain territorial superiority or merely to assert their status in the heirarchy of local elephant populations.

Tactile contact between individuals is a highly important aspect of social interaction, and helps to develop strong bonds between family members. In addition to other functions such as eating and drinking, elephants use their sensitive trunks to touch, caress, shove and sniff their companions.

Painted golden by late afternoon sunlight, a family of elephants led by a tuskless cow (*above*) emerges from the river after their evening drink. While elephants frequently break their tusks either during feeding or fighting, it is becoming increasingly common throughout Africa for both bulls and cows to fail to grow tusks – perhaps a genetic response to the singling out of the biggest and best tuskers in elephant populations by both legal and illegal hunters. Invariably such animals seem to be more irascible and aggressive, probably as a direct result of having no defensive weapons!

The dense riverine vegetation along the Uaso Nyiro River (*left*) provides both shelter and nutrition for elephants, as well as for a large variety of smaller mammals and bird life. Elephants are mixed feeders and vary their diets considerably between coarse dry sticks, bark and branches, succulent roots and fruits, and tender shoots and leaves. Although the wide sweep of the Uaso Nyiro River forms a natural boundary between Samburu and Buffalo Springs national reserves, it presents no obstacle to the passage of elephants who cross from one side to the other at will. Turbid and slow-moving here, the river has its origins in the heights of the Aberdare Mountains and plummets over the spectacular Thomson's Falls before slowing its pace as it crosses the Samburu flatlands. Downstream it gains momentum once more, plunging down the Sharinki Falls and through deep rocky gorges on its journey to the Lorian swamps.

# MASAI MARA
# NATIONAL RESERVE

A pastoral landscape of gently undulating grasslands set against the towering backdrop of the Siria Escarpment, 'the Mara' is one of earth's most visually stunning wildscapes. Forming the northernmost part of the vast Serengeti-Mara ecosystem, Kenya's Masai Mara is the canvas across which one of the greatest natural spectacles on the planet pours each year, when the annual migration of wildebeest, zebra and several antelope species sees as many as 2,2 million animals flooding on to its vast golden grasslands from neighbouring Serengeti. For four months of every year, this migration is the focus of attention on the Mara, though the reserve boasts abundant – and visible – populations of elephant, big cats including lion, leopard and cheetah, as well as buffalo, giraffe and plains species such as topi, kongoni, Thomson's and Grant's gazelle, and zebra, while both black and newly reintroduced white rhino are thriving. Through the year the Mara sustains nearly 1,5 million animals – the greatest concentration in Africa.

The 1 500-square-kilometre park has experienced a dramatic increase in its elephant population since the 1960s, with the animals attracted by the lush, fertile plains covered with nutritious red oatgrass (*far right*), wet swampy areas such as those around the Musiara marsh, and rich riverine forests (*right*) which fringe the Mara River. Poaching in the nearby country of Tanzania and human habitation on the reserve's borders have further served to put pressure on elephants and numbers in the reserve have soared from from 500 in the 1970s to 1 500 today.

Draping his trunk across a young cow's back, a Mara bull tests her receptiveness and readiness for mating (*opposite top*). On encountering a breeding herd, a male will usually move from cow to cow looking for a suitable mate, only linking up with the herd when a female comes into oestrus. At this stage he will generally have to compete with other bulls for the right to mate, which often results in violent clashes. Although males reach sexual maturity at about 12 years of age, they usually only begin to compete for the right to mate around the age of 25, and even then they are not as successful as the fully mature adults.

Bulls in musth, a physiological and psychological state of heightened sexual excitement and aggression thought to be associated with high levels of the male hormone testosterone, are usually the most successful of all. The females are also often highly selective and will avoid certain males, usually choosing the biggest, strongest and 'best looking' of the available musth bulls. Mating (*above and opposite bottom*) generally takes place over several days, during which time the courting couple will stay together in 'consortship', the female never moving further than a few metres from her partner.

Elephant calves (*above*) have few concerns in life: in their first few months they rarely move beyond a few trunk-lengths of their mother and are closely cared for by elder sisters, aunts and other herd members as they go about their daily frolics.

A large bull lies down for a post-coitive rest (*opposite top and bottom*) following successful mating with an oestrus cow, while several junior members of the herd lie in a close huddle. Elephant copulations are usually accompanied by much excitement and agitation within the herd, particularly among younger members, while the actual mating appears to be exhausting for both the cow and the bull. However, it is unusual for the bull to join the calves like this, sleeping prone and exposed in the open. Elephants commonly sleep for short periods standing upright.

Feeding almost continuously through day and night, an adult elephant (*above*) will consume as much as 200 kilograms of food in a 24-hour period, adapting its diet to whatever food is most readily available. The succulent grasses fringing the Musiara marsh in the northern region of the Mara provide soft, easily digested fodder.

After the main rains in April–May, and again in October–November, the rolling plains of the Mara (*right*) are covered with a carpet of lush, nutritious grasses much favoured by both elephants and the vast herds of migrating animals that throng here after their journey from Tanzania's Serengeti National Park. Through the night and during the cooler hours of the day the elephants will move on to the grasslands to feed.

# AMBOSELI
# NATIONAL PARK

Mount Kilimanjaro (*right*) lies just south of Kenya's border with Tanzania, with its snow-capped peaks and glacier-covered summit standing like a surreal beacon in the midst of heat-hazed African plains. Kilimanjaro is one of the great mountains of the world, rising in splendid isolation 5 895 metres over the surrounding landscape. The majestic mountain presides over the almost totally flat, open plains and dry lake-bed of Amboseli National Park, with waters from its melting glaciers feeding the cool, clear springs that in turn sustain the succulent grasses and marshes that nourish as many as 700 elephants throughout the year.

Although Amboseli's once thriving black rhino population almost disappeared entirely during the height of large-scale commercial poaching operations some years ago, the resident elephants have escaped largely unscathed. Amboseli's elephants have experienced neither significant hunting nor culling, and this, together with a relatively high number of tourist operators in the park, has resulted in animals that are remarkably approachable and unconcerned by human proximity. The open habitat, amenable elephants and spectacular backdrop make for the quintessential elephant photographs, though the mountain is frequently invisible, shrouded in dense cloud and mist.

An elephant's trunk (*right*) can weigh as much as two grown men. A versatile and essential tool, it nevertheless often appears to become quite burdensome to its owner, who will frequently drape it casually over a tusk to ease the load.

Although Amboseli falls in the rainshadow of Mount Kilimanjaro and experiences frequent droughts, its perennial springs and underground waterways are the lifeblood of the park and result in the good grazing that attracts numerous herbivores such as these elephant *(above)*, as well as herds of wildebeest and zebra.

When darkness falls in Amboseli most of the elephants move off the plains and head into the surrounding woodlands, wandering across the international border into Tanzania and towards the lower slopes of Kilimanjaro *(left)*. Here they utilise feeding areas not available to them during the day because of the presence of Maasai herdsmen and their cattle, and perhaps they also feel more secure away from the open plains at night. The next morning the herds return to the lowlands to take advantage of the long, soft grasses in and around the swampy marshes. Sadly several well-known Amboseli bull elephants have fallen under the guns of unscrupulous professional hunters here lately, despite a Tanzanian government ban on shooting elephants in this region.

Two elephant calves, probably closely related cousins, gain security and comfort from their proximity to one another while playing in the shadow of an adult cow, most likely the mother of the smaller calf. Elephant cows are extremely protective of both their own young and those of other family members and can be aggressive and dangerous when young calves are about.

Elephants enjoy close family relationships particularly in matri-
archal herds, and it is not unusual for them to rest, feed, drink or
move about in tightly bunched groups touching flank to flank as if
to signal to one another 'It's nice to have you with me!' Young calves
in particular never stray far from their mother's side.

Pushing and shoving, young bull elephants (*opposite and above*) jostle for dominance in a vigorous juvenile sparring session. Such behaviour will continue through puberty, gaining in severity and seriousness as they get older. Adult elephants often damage their tusks when they clash, sustain tears to their ears or other minor injuries, although more serious injuries are rare. While real fights between adult bulls are frightening in their intensity and fury, few fatalities have been recorded as one of the protagonists will usually back down and retreat before blood is spilled.

Amboseli's handsome elephants (*previous page*) are some of the most serene and least disturbed we encountered as they have never been culled and poaching is rare.

# TSAVO
# NATIONAL RESERVE

Kenya's largest protected wilderness area, Tsavo is one of the great game reserves of the world. Wild, untamed and prone to harsh, unpredictable weather patterns, it was once home to over 45 000 elephants until first drought in the 1960s and then unprecedented ivory poaching in the 1970s and 1980s – primarily by heavily armed gangs of Somali 'shifta' bandits – slashed that figure to fewer than 6 000. Fortunately, since the ban on trading in ivory in 1989, allied with anti-poaching patrols, Tsavo's elephant population has made a resurgence and even black rhino, reintroduced after illegal hunters totally wiped them out, are on the increase.

In the late 1960s and early 1970s, Tsavo was the focus of a controversial experiment when the park wardens rejected plans to cull elephants to reduce pressure on the park's vegetation. The resulting 'devastation' of the once thickly-wooded park, allied with the effects of a severe drought in 1970–74, transformed Tsavo into open grasslands attracting large herds of herbivores such as zebra and wildebeest and their attendant predators. Today gameviewing can be spectacular and the park is a major earner of tourist revenue.

Famous for its 'pink elephants' *(right and below)* – a colour which results from their wallowing in the predominantly red soils of the region – the park is divided into two administrative sectors, East and West, by the main route linking Nairobi and the port of Mombasa on the Indian Ocean coast. Tsavo East has become home to a number of elephants reintroduced from Daphne Sheldrick's elephant orphanage outside Nairobi. They have been assisted in their rehabilitation by skilled handlers and the attentions of the matriarch Eleanor, herself once a hand-reared orphan who was reintroduced to the wilds of the park, who has taken it upon herself to act as a foster-mother to new arrivals.

Mud-wallowing and bathing, particularly in the hot, dry months, are important daily activities which, apart from serving to protect elephants from parasites, insects and the sun, also appear to afford them simple pleasure and joy. Young calves roll and wallow with total abandon and, like human children, appear reluctant to leave when the time comes for the herd to move on.

Elephants drink from the Voi River near the park headquarters in Tsavo East *(opposite)*. They need as much as 200 litres of water a day and prefer fresh, clean water such as that provided by swiftly flowing rivers or fresh rainwater pans. Paradoxically elephants will readily foul their drinking source by defecating and urinating in it or bathing and churning up the muddy bottom.

A herd of Cape buffalo *(Syncerus caffer)* and elephants mingle at the waterhole below Voi Safari Lodge in Tsavo East *(left)*, with the flat expanse of the park stretching away into the distance. While most elephants will usually tolerate other animals around them, if water availability is poor they will exclude other game from the waterholes until they have drunk their fill.

Large herds *(left)* are usually made up of several smaller family units that have gathered together for short periods of social interaction. Elephants tend to confine themselves to smaller family units for most of the time, only gathering into large aggregations when feeding conditions are good, or in times of stress.

# TARANGIRE
# NATIONAL PARK

Monolithic, ancient baobabs stud the gently rolling plains of Tanzania's Tarangire National Park *(right)* and create a landscape uniquely African and distinctly prehistoric, dwarfing even the majestic stature of the elephants. During the dry months, Tarangire, covering an area of about 2 600 square kilometres, attracts large numbers of elephants and huge herds of plains species (wildebeest, zebra, buffalo, eland and oryx). Drawn by the permanent waters of the Tarangire River and the nutritious grazing provided by the grassy acacia parkland and riverine woodlands, game concentrations are rivalled only by those in the Ngorongoro Crater area to the north. Although umbrella and fever trees also add their striking presence to the landscape, it is the vast numbers of massive, clustered baobabs that make Tarangire's scenery so remarkable.

The park's elephant population fluctuates considerably with the seasons: during the rains most of them will be widely scattered over more than 20 000 square kilometres of the southern Maasai steppe to the south and east, while in the dry season, which runs from July through to October, as many as 3 000 will return to the area and groups of bulls, breeding herds and family units like this cow and her young calf *(right)* can be seen.

Tarangire was one of the surprise discoveries of our four-year elephant research project. Its stunning scenery, spectacular baobab trees, high elephant population and low tourist density make it one of East Africa's unspoilt destinations.

Elephants throng daily to the waters of the perennial Tarangire River (*right*), the only permanent water to in the entire region. Flowing through the length of the park from south to north, the river ends its long journey in Lake Burungi, a shallow soda lake just outside the park's northwestern boundary. Her drinking done, an elephant cow naps quietly at the water's edge, her trunk coiled casually across her tusks (*below*).

Tarangire's most striking features are its majestic ancient baobabs, at their most prolific in the northern triangle of the park known as Lemiyon *(above)*. Elephants regularly feed on the soft, fibrous stems and nutritious bark of these trees *(opposite)*, particularly before the rains bring relief to the countryside at the end of the dry season. They will frequently eat holes right though the massive trunks and have been known to topple them completely.

# NGORONGORO
# CONSERVATION AREA

The earth's largest volcanic caldera, Ngorongoro Crater is rightfully regarded as one of the natural wonders of the world. Formed over two million years ago, it has been sculptured by time into a fertile, lush oasis of swamp, savannah and acacia forest. Today it supports an extraordinary array of wildlife, the 260-square kilometre crater floor being home to a resident population of as many as 25 000 large mammals – although elephants are present only in limited numbers.

While several large old bulls appear to have taken up permanent residence and about 70 others regularly come and go, breeding herds rarely descend to the crater floor as the steep, and in places heavily wooded, 600-metre-high crater walls are perhaps too great an obstacle for small calves, particularly on the climb back out.

No safari to East Africa would be complete without a visit to Tanzania's spectacular Ngorongoro Crater, which, while not home to a particularly large elephant population, provides a setting that is unequalled anywhere. Because of a high volume of tourist traffic the crater's animals are vehicle-tolerant and close-up photographic opportunities are virtually guaranteed.

The Ngorongoro Conservation Area is famous for its black rhino and lion, while, in addition to its resident elephants, other herbivores such as Coke's hartebeest, zebra and wildebeest abound, along with their attendant predators.

Sunlight breaking through a gap in the cloud cover illuminates a section of the Lerai Forest and a scattering of wildebeest and zebra grazing the short-grass plains (*right*). Wildebeest and zebra comprise the bulk of the game population on the crater floor, their numbers fluctuating between 5 000 and 15 000, depending on conditions.

Elephants play a vital role in the grazing succession among the coarse grasses which grow along the edges of the springs and swamps of the crater floor (*below*). By cropping the grasses short and trampling them into the mud they allow them to sprout again, allowing the tender new shoots preferred by the wildebeest and gazelles to grow.

An elderly elephant, readily identifiable by his floppy ear, *(left)* feeds contentedly alongside several gnarled old fever trees *(Acacia xanthophloea)* adjacent to the fringes of the Gorigor swamp.

Rearing up on his hind legs like a circus animal, an elephant bull stretches to the utmost to reach the fresh acacia shoots in the Lerai forest *(below)*.

# MANA POOLS
# NATIONAL PARK

Egrets swirl and scatter in the path of a towering bull elephant feeding across the broad riverine flood plain of Zimbabwe's Mana Pools National Park, while the darkly brooding Zambezi escarpment on the Zambian side of the river throws the scene into stark relief *(right)*. Mana Pools is known for its big elephant bulls and beautiful woodland setting in the Zambezi Valley, where the mighty river and impressive escarpment create a unique African landscape.

Late evening sunlight casts a soft golden glow down the length of the valley, gilding a lone bull elephant as it enjoys a quiet sundowner at the riverside *(below)*. As the dry season lengthens, more and more elephants arrive at the riverfront, retreating from the arid hinterland to take advantage of the Zambezi's perennial waters and the nutritious browse provided by the albida woodlands.

Mana's elephants are renowned for their circus-like antics of rearing up on their hind legs to reach the seedpods and tender new growth of the towering albida woodlands on the river's flood plain. Organised poaching gangs infiltrating the country from neighbouring Zambia have annihilated the park's formerly healthy black rhino population and now the elephants are coming under increasing pressure, though Mana is still one of the best places for exceptional elephant viewing.

Mana Pools is perhaps the only park in Africa containing the Big Five where visitors are allowed to walk at will, unaccompanied by armed rangers.

Open wide . . . An elephant's jaw gapes wide open while it reaches with its trunk high over its head to feed *(opposite)*. Elephants wear down up to six sets of molars during their lifetime; after the last set wears out, they have difficulty eating and gradually lose condition, ultimately dying of starvation.

The lofty mature woodland of the lower Zambezi Valley flood plain is highly favoured by the elephant population, which must stretch and reach high to feed on the tender topmost shoots and nutritious seedpods of the tall albida thorn trees *(right)*.

Like most acacia species to which it is closely related, the pods of *Faidherbia albida*, also known as the apple-ring because of the shape of its seed-pods *(above)*, are highly nutritious and much sought after by a wide variety of animals. Elephants, giraffes and baboons can reach them where they grow, while antelope like kudu and impala must rely on those that drop to the ground.

A herd of elephants crosses the Zambezi River shortly after sunrise (*above*), returning from the Zambian side of the river to the relative safety of the shores in Mana Pools National Park in Zimbabwe. Elephants appear to have an instinctive knowledge of where they are in danger from poachers or hunters.

A lone elephant feeds peacefully on lush forest grasses, apparently dwarfed by the statuesque albidas towering overhead (*left*). The dapple-shaded Mana Pools woodlands attract large herds of buffalo and other ungulates, as well as the predators that prey upon them. The elephants for which the park is justly famous are at their most evident during the dry season.

An elephant stretches to feed on the lush riverine vegetation that lines the banks of the life-giving waters of the Zambezi River, the fourth largest river in Africa, which forms the boundary between Zambia in the north and Zimbabwe in the south. It is this abundance of vegetation that attracts a wealth of wildlife to the area.

Taking a break from the riverfront and its accompanying woodlands, an elephant feeds upon succulent aquatic plants growing across the surface of a pan some way back from the Zambezi. The park gets its name from the large, semi-permanent pools that, except in the worst of dry years, hold water throughout the seasons.

Dust hangs in a heavy pall as a breeding herd of elephants rushes through thick jesse scrub and woodland on their way to the riverside (*above*). Breeding herds with young are more easily panicked than the more placid bulls. The matriarch will lead the herd to water, allowing her charges to quench their thirst quickly, before moving them on to the relative safety of the surrounding woodland.

A ray of sun highlights a portion of an elephant bull's head and tusks as he rests in the shade of a large tree (*opposite*). Mana Pools is home to number of elephant bulls who are quite undisturbed by the close proximity of man.

# MATUSADONA
# NATIONAL PARK

Nestled along the southern shoreline of Lake Kariba in the shadow of the steeply rising Matusadona range, this is a park of wide-ranging contrasts, from the broad, open lakeside flats through dense mopane woodland and rock-strewn, rugged mountain slopes. One of the largest man-made lakes in the world, Kariba flooded vast tracts of indigenous Zambezi valley woodland, trapping countless animals on ever-diminishing islands as the waters rose. This led to Operation Noah, the largest and most heroic animal-rescue operation ever undertaken, with volunteers led by Rupert Fothergill working day and night to trap and capture a myriad stranded animals and release them on the mainland in the vicinity of today's Matusadona National Park. Superb swimmers, the elephants continued for many years to follow ancient footpaths criss-crossing the newly flooded valley floor, swimming huge distances across this vast inland sea in search of their traditional feeding grounds.

Nowadays the elephants seem atuned to the loss of their former range and sightings of them swimming far out in the lake are infrequent. Instead they seek out the lush lakeshore grasses (*far right*) that are exposed when the high water levels recede during the dry season. Along the lake's edge stand the skeletal remains of dead trees drowned by the rising waters (*right*).

Matusadona National Park can be relied upon for some spectacular sunrises and sunsets over Lake Kariba, as well as large numbers of elephants which feed and bathe along the water's edge. Once home to the legendary Karonga bull, Zimbabwe's largest tusker which was killed in a fight with a younger rival, Matusadona is still home to some of the country's biggest elephants.

Ears flared and trunk flailing, an elephant draws itself up to its full height in typical 'mock charge' pose, attempting, with success, to appear as intimidating as possible *(above)*.

The steep escarpment of the Matusadona range fills the background as an elephant strolls past a small inlet *(right)*. Skeletal trees, killed when rising lake waters drowned their root systems, are a feature of the Kariba shoreline.

While elephants frequently break their tusks when establishing their dominance or in using them to create mud-wallows or to dig for water, occasionally they will lose an entire tusk from the root up, like this elephant we saw in Matusadona (*above*). It is not known what causes this affliction – perhaps it is an abscess or similar dental problem – but it is unlikely that this tusk will regenerate, as opposed to a broken tusk which will continue to grow until it regains its full size.

The typically wasted lower trunk of the 'floppy trunk disease' that began to manifest itself among Kariba and lower Zambezi Valley elephants in the early 1990s is evident in this elephant (*opposite*) as it wades through a shallow Kariba lagoon. The causes of the ailment have not yet been diagnosed, though some theories point to an organic toxin that is ingested by the elephants feeding on an as yet unidentified plant.

# HWANGE
# NATIONAL PARK

Zimbabwe's largest national park, Hwange is home to an elephant population measured in the tens of thousands rather than hundreds, although the exact population at any one time is a matter of some conjecture as the herds move freely from the park into Botswana. Like most of the parks in the more arid areas of southern Africa, it is around the waterholes that much of the elephant activity takes place, with large herds thronging to them to cool off during the heat of the day, and later on to drink towards sundown. While large breeding herds with young calves generally spend little time at the water, particularly in places where they have been disturbed by human conflict, hunting and culling, the bulls appear to take much pleasure in their lengthy visits to waterholes where they enjoy socialising with other males *(below)*.

Although elephants can go for several days without water, they generally need to drink daily, consuming up to 200 litres a day. They use their dextrous trunks to drink, adults easily siphoning up to 18 litres at a time, then squirting it into their mouths *(right)*.

In recent years, however, the country's cash-strapped economy and administrative problems have lead to many of the park's borehole pumps breaking down or running out of fuel; this is turn has resulted in waterholes drying out and elephants moving away from the area. Private censuses of Hwange National Park's elephant population seriously question official figures, though it is possible that the large elephant herds have become more migratory in response to the unreliability of the water supplies.

Dust-bathing *(above)* is generally associated with other social activities that occur around the waterhole and is often accompanied by physical contact such as caressing, trunk-entwining and sparring between younger bulls. A thick coating of dust, frequently layered over a covering of mud from an earlier wallow, helps to keep parasites like ticks and biting flies in check and is also thought to play a role in thermo-regulation.

Dust flies during the late afternoon as an elephant herd breaks into a quick-stepping shuffle approaching one of Hwange's many man-made waterholes *(left)*. Cow herds such as this will generally visit water only once a day, often traversing large distances to and from their feeding range to do so, and will drink their fill without delay before retreating to the thick scrub. In contrast to the quick visits by cow herds, elephant bulls seem to delight in prolonging their stays at drinking holes, revelling in the social interaction with other bulls and using every opportunity to exercise their hierarchical dominance. Younger, inferior bulls will often have to stand back for lengthy periods, awaiting their chance to drink once the elders have finished.

An adult elephant guarding the rest of the herd steps out as dark storm clouds gather in the distance. Strange as it may seem, elephants are exceptionally well camouflaged against the dull browns of the bushveld vegetation and these large animals are able to disappear from view in an instant. Elephants are known to influence their environment by felling large trees and by modifying habitats to suit other animals. An example of this is the practice of elephants opening bushy thickets which over the years became transformed into grassland savannah, increasing grazing opportunities for antelope and other ungulates.

# KRUGER
# NATIONAL PARK

The flagship of South African conservation, at 22 000-plus square kilometres in extent, Kruger is also one of the largest game reserves in Africa and without doubt the most highly developed and intensively managed. Known for some of Africa's biggest tuskers, Kruger's elephant population has been maintained at a constant population of about 7 500 animals by a comprehensive annual culling programme which aimed to 'take off' the equivalent of the annual breeding increment.

This policy is, however, under review, as the authorities monitor the carrying capacity of the park and examine whether the surplus population can be managed by the translocation of elephant family units to other reserves or by purchasing additional land adjacent to Kruger. As a result of the culling, cow herds are infrequently sighted, since these animals generally prefer to remain in dense cover during the day and drinking by night. Bulls, however, are commonly encountered along most of the tourist roads throughout the park, although it is the dense mopane veld (*far right*) in the northern parts of the park around rest camps such as Olifants, Letaba and Shingwedzi that is particularly noted for its large elephant populations as well as its big tuskers.

Several private reserves adjoin the western boundary of the Kruger National Park; a recent move to abolish fences between the park and these reserves allows the elephants to move at will.

Mandleve was the most recent of Kruger's truly great tuskers to roam the park *(opposite)*. He died peacefully of old age several months after these photographs were taken. His tusks, both in the 60-kilogram class, can be seen on display in the 'Elephant Hall' museum in Letaba Rest Camp.

Mandleve rests in the midday heat of the Sabi Sabi Game Reserve adjoining Kruger National Park, his 'askaris' or attendants maintaining a vigilant watch *(above)*. Old bulls will often be accompanied by younger males who act as lookouts to compensate for the older animal's failing senses, but benefiting from their charge's greater knowledge and experience. The Swahili word 'askari' means policeman or guard.

With remarkable dexterity, an elephant first breaks a section of bark free with a probing tusk (*above*), then peels it back with its trunk (*left*). Elephant regularly debark trees and shrubs as part of their diet, although studies indicate that bark does not make up a high proportion of their daily food intake. Comprising as many as 50 000 muscle units the versatile trunk can perform such delicate tasks as extracting a thorn from a foot pad, removing mud from an eye . . . or smashing trees out of the earth.

Highly sought-after by collectors, trophy hunters and curio-carvers, heavy ivory such as that carried by this old tusker in the Kruger Park (*opposite*) has resulted in the demise of similar bulls throughout most of Africa, gunned down by both legal and illegal hunters in senseless slaughter fuelled primarily by greed.

Dust flies as a charging bull skids to a halt (*opposite*) in the intimidating mock charge posture. This elephant, frequently seen in the Lower Sabie area, is one of the new generation of big tuskers in the park.

Taking advantage of an area of loose soil an elephant (*above*) indulges in an impromptu dustbathing session while feeding in thick mopane scrub, the dominant vegetation in the northern region of the park which is an area frequented by many of Kruger's large tuskers.

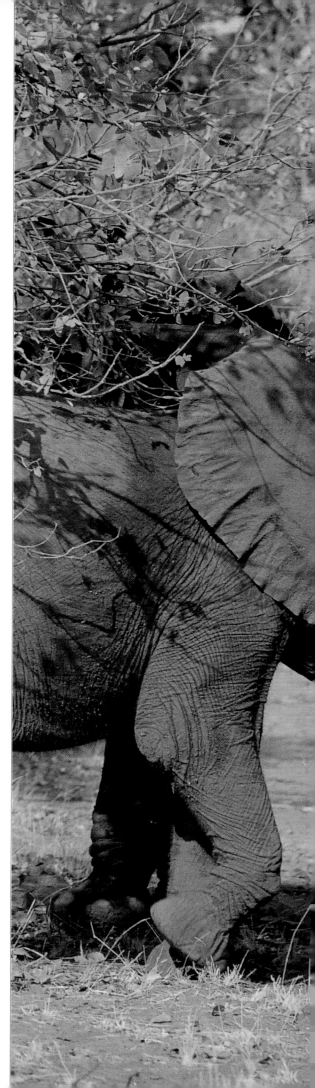

A young elephant takes refuge amid a forest of trunks and legs as its mother and elder siblings attempt to screen it from perceived danger *(above)*. Baby elephants generally have few cares in the world, and this one blissfully continued its investigation of a heap of fresh dung while its family, feeling threatened by the proximity of our vehicle, huddled around it *(right)*.

Elephants feed peacefully on lush riverine growth and water hyacinth growing along the edge of the Letaba River in the northern sector of the park *(overleaf)*.

# ADDO ELEPHANT NATIONAL PARK

Situated about 72 kilometres north of Port Elizabeth, Addo was proclaimed in 1931 after concerted efforts by both local farmers and Major Philip Pretorius, commissioned by the government to eliminate elephants altogether from the area, had failed. By this time only 11 elephants were left, concealed by the extensive, impenetrable thorn thickets covering much of the area. Contrary to former belief these elephant, along with a remnant population in the Knysna forests further south, are of the same sub-species as their more northern kin. They are the sole survivors of the great herds that once roamed the southern Cape as recently as the latter half of the 19th century. Although protected within the newly established park, the remaining elephants continued to raid nearby crops and as a result were constantly harassed by the local farmers. Some 20 years later Graham Armstrong perfected an elephant-proof fence made of thick cables and stout posts constructed from elevator cables and old tram lines. Completed in 1954, it was called the Armstrong fence in his honour.

Though relatively small, Addo embraces one of the highest concentrations of big game in Africa. Today about 170 elephants populate the park, which was considerably enlarged from its original 2 270 to 12 126 hectares (recently the undeveloped Zuurberg National Park was incorporated into Addo, but at this stage there are no elephants in this section). Addo bulls are typified by their small stature and insignificant tusks (*right and far right*); the cows are all tuskless, apart from three known animals. Sharing the densely vegetated park are a herd of the only remaining naturally occurring buffalo in the Cape region, as well as more than 25 of the scarce Kenyan sub-species of black rhinoceros, *Diceros bicornis michaeli*.

About 80 percent of Addo is covered by the 'spekboom' (*Portulacaria afra*) which occurs in tangled thickets much loved by elephants (*left*) as fodder and cover.

The small tusks carried by the Addo elephants (*top*) are thought to be the result of selective hunting of the large tuskers during the 19th century, resulting in only those with genetically small ivory surviving to breed.

Addo is the last refuge of the flightless dung beetle (*Circellium bacchus*) (*above*).

# KAOKOVELD

A region encompassing Damaraland and Kaokoland in Namibia's arid and isolated northwestern corner, the Kaokoveld is perhaps one of the last places on the African continent in which one would expect to find elephants. Yet this dry, dusty, rock-strewn desert landscape of towering volcanic escarpments, dry river courses, windblown sand dunes and sparsely vegetated plains and plateaux is home to the famed 'desert elephants' (below). The small but apparently thriving population has adapted itself to its harsh surroundings, feeding conservatively and sparingly on the region's trees and shrubs and trekking long distances to find water only every three or four days, unlike elephants in other areas which are more destructive while they feed and which normally drink on a daily basis.

Although a number of rivers traverse the region, none are perennial; most flow above ground only briefly after occasional summer rains and many remain dry riverbeds for years at a time. Water-dependent wildlife, such as the desert-dwelling elephants and the equally famous black rhinos and giraffe, make use of a number of isolated springs, reservoirs and oases, such as that at Palmwag in Damaraland (far right), where they frequently visit to drink and feed on the lush vegetation fringing the natural spring.

Because of the vastness of the elephants' territory and the harshness of their habitat, only a fraction of their range is protected, falling under the Skeleton Coast National Park. This is a matter of some concern as more and more people flock to the region, either to graze their livestock or merely as tourists who wish to venture off the beaten track.

Although its distinctly unusual habitat might suggest it, the desert-dwelling elephant *(above)* is not a separate sub-species of the African elephant, but in fact belongs to the same sub-species as the common savannah elephant that ranges over most of east, central and southern Africa, *Loxodonta africana africana*. Like the Addo and Knysna elephants of the Cape, they are however classified as an ecotype – a population that differs from others by being adapted to their habitat by diet, behaviour, tradition and possibly physiology. Bulls, as well as cows and their families, occupy home ranges several times larger than those occupied by elephants in less arid areas.

The barren, lunar landscape of rock and desert dune forms a surreal setting for any elephant *(left)*. It is one of the most inhospitable habitats on the African continent.

His ears flared in annoyance at the photographer's intrusion into his domain, a lone bull strides along a rock-littered section of the dry Hoanib riverbed in Kaokoland (*above*). Because resources in this area are scarce, desert-dwelling elephants spend a great deal of time and energy on the move, in search of food and water. They are able to locate water sources many kilometres away across the harshest of desert environments, a profound knowledge which is passed down from one generation to another (*right*).

# ETOSHA
# NATIONAL PARK

Known as the 'great white place', Namibia's Etosha was the largest conservation area in the world until it was cut back to its present 22 270 square kilometres in 1967, yet it still remains one of the greatest and most fascinating sanctuaries in Africa. Noted for its huge and diverse herds of game that in the dry winter season throng to the park's limited number of permanent waterpoints, Etosha has a large and thriving elephant population well habituated to human presence and readily viewed throughout the park. The growth of the elephant herds has been particularly dramatic: from fewer than 100 individuals in the 1950s, there are now about 2 500.

As is the case with the majority of other game species in Etosha, the waterholes in the park are the best place to observe elephants in all their different moods and activities. There can be few sights as exciting to watch as a large breeding herd coming down to drink, the adults huge and stately while the juniors splash and frolic about their feet.

Etosha's elephants have not experienced much of the poaching that decimated other elephant populations in Africa, as their tusks are too brittle and of poor quality. Culling in the reserve was suspended a number of years back, leaving undisturbed herds with the result that cows and their calves, such as these enjoying a mud-bath (*far right*), can be observed at all times of the day and at relatively close quarters.

In a touching display of emotion, a young bull chases scavenging vultures from the carcass of a dead elephant – in all probability a fallen family member. Elephants are known to display a deep sensitivity and awareness of death and will return repeatedly to carcasses and skeletons of deceased herd members, running their trunks gently over the remains as though paying their respects.

An older bull straddles a fallen comrade, attempting to shield his head from the harsh overhead sun while offering water with his trunk. We watched spellbound for several hours after the elephant had first staggered, then fallen, unable to rise again, most likely a victim of the killer bacterial disease anthrax which destroys many animals in Etosha each year. His companion first tried to raise him, lifting him with trunk and tusks to no avail, then brought water from the nearby spring which he sprayed over the dying elephant's head and ears and tried to get him to drink.

Waterholes serve as places of social interaction for groups of elephants which may not otherwise come into contact (*above*), and single animals will often loiter in the vicinity of such places until other elephants arrive (*left*). Elephants spend as many as 18 to 20 hours a day feeding and drinking, though they will generally only visit water once in this period except in extremely hot and dry conditions. During Etosha's wetter summer months – the 'green season' – it is uncommon to find elephants visiting waterholes at all, since they are able to utilise seasonal pools and puddles filled by occasional rainstorms.

Etosha's elephants have escaped the greed-fuelled slaughter experienced in much of Africa, largely because they have stunted, brittle tusks *(right)* as a result of calcium and phosphate deficiencies in their diet, making the ivory of little value to the carving industry. Because of their fragile nature the tusks are often broken off *(above)* as a result of feuding and sparring between bulls, as well as when digging for roots and tubers.

The floodlit waterhole at Etosha's main camp, Okaukuejo, is one of the main attractions and a popular place to see elephants, which come and go continuously through the day and night (*above*). It is not unusual to see elephant nonchalantly quenching their thirst or browsing on thorn scrub only a few metres away

The colour of Etosha's famed 'white elephants' (*opposite*) is the result of their wallowing in the white calcrete clay on the edges of the vast, salt encrusted pan, centrepiece of this large reserve.

# SAVUTI

Located at the heart of Botswana's Chobe National Park, Savuti is big bull territory. Dusty, dry and windblown for much of the year, it was once a lush, green swampland fed by the waters of the Savuti Channel, which originated in the Linyanti Swamps, then wound its way in a south-easterly direction before finally disappearing into the Mababe Depression. Due to tectonic upheaval deep within the earth's crust, the channel ceased flowing in 1981 and the Savuti marsh shrivelled and dried, leaving the dead skeletons of camelthorn trees scattered across the desolate plains. Many of the animals that resided here trekked north and deserted the area for good, although some, like the huge herds of migrating zebra, wildebeest and buffalo, still return annually in summer after the onset of soaking rains when the grasslands are restored to their former beauty.

In an effort to bring some dry-season relief to the wildlife of the region, boreholes have been sunk in the vicinity of the marsh and several man-made waterholes developed, the most famous of these being Pump Pan, frequented by a large cross-section of game, such as this impala herd sharing the water with a lone bull elephant *(right and below)*. It is here that tourists in open-topped safari vehicles can enjoy spectacular eyeball to eyeball encounters with these placid giants, frequently numbering as many as 50 or 60 as they jostle for water.

Apart from the large numbers of elephant bulls that inhabit the area, Savuti is also renowned for its concentration of predators, particularly lions, which generally regard these old bulls with some degree of caution. Although breeding herds of elephant are not often seen in this area, those that do occasionally pass through have been known to lose calves to mau-rauding prides of lions, which are adept at hunting big game animals such as buffalo.

Seeking relief from the burning sun, a trio of elephants (*above*) shelter in the shade of a camelthorn tree (*Acacia erioloba*). One of the dominant tree species of the area, it provides both shelter and sustenance, as its nutritious, protein-rich seedpods are much favoured by elephants, as well as other browsers such as kudu and giraffe. A fork in the trunk of a camelthorn provides a handy spot to wedge a tusk, supporting the weight of an elephant's head as it sleeps contentedly in the shade (*opposite*). An elephant generally sleeps for only three or four hours a day. Very occasionally it may lie down for an hour or so, but mostly it takes short, cumulative naps, usually standing upright or, as here, leaning against a tree.

Bull elephants *(top and right)* come to drink at a rain-filled pan on the otherwise dry, flat expanse of the Savuti marsh, as a large flock of Burchell's sandgrouse *(Pterocles burchelli)* lands at the waters' edge. Only the sandgrouse males *(above)* have absorbent breast feathers specially evolved to aid them in carrying water to nest-bound chicks, often as much as 50 or 60 kilometres away from the water.

A bull elephant *(overleaf)* trudges wearily across the eastern side of the Savuti marsh, an early summer sky promising the dramatic onset of the season's rains.

Although predators such as these wild dogs (*left*) and lion (*above*) pose no threat to an adult elephant, most elephants are intolerant of them and will chase them aggressively. Savuti is renowned for its large predator population, especially for its large lion prides and high concentration of hyaena, but leopard and wild dog are also fairly common. Wild dogs are endangered throughout Africa, although Botswana has a healthy population.

# CHOBE NATIONAL PARK

Botswana boasts a burgeoning elephant population of more than 71 500, with most of these being found in the 12 000-square-kilometre Chobe National Park, located in the far northeast of the country. The subject of much debate by ecologists and environmentalists over recent years, this huge population is believed by some to be far in excess of the region's carrying capacity. They point to the 'destruction' of the riverine vegetation along the Chobe riverfront as their proof – notwithstanding the fact that the original forest here was subjected to intensive logging operations until as recently as a few decades ago. Irrespective of these opposing opinions, the Chobe riverfront is today one of the best places in Africa to observe and photograph large herds of elephants, particularly in the dry season when the broad flood plains can be covered with many hundreds of elephants in the late afternoons.

Although biologists are divided on the issue of whether there are too many elephant in Chobe for the habitat to sustain, what is certain is that should culling operations begin here, as some have proposed, elephant viewing will never be the same again.

The Linyanti Swamp, another prime elephant habitat, lies in a westerly direction. In this corner of the Chobe National Park and the adjacent private Selinda Game Reserve sanctuary is provided for the more vulnerable breeding herds during the dry season.

One of the unforgettable sights in Chobe is that of the sun sinking in a molten red orb behind a herd of elephants peacefully going about their evening activities *(far right)*. While most herds return to the woodlands further inland after drinking and bathing *(right)*, some remain feeding on the flood plains through the night.

Chobe is justly famous for its riverfront activities and a highlight of most visits to the park is a late afternoon boat cruise which allows visitors to the park to observe elephants from close quarters (*top and above*). This is the time that massed elephant herds throng to the river to bathe and quench their thirst, and some take part in raiding parties, swimming across the river shortly before sunset (*right*) to spend the night feeding in the maize fields on the Namibian side.

Practically obscured in a cloud of dust, a family of elephants (*above*) dust-bathe after wallowing in a pool at the head of the Savuti Channel in the Linyanti region of Chobe.

Although there is generally little more than a tenuous truce and reluctant acceptance of each other's presence at a waterhole, hippos and elephants usually have little to do with one another. However, in this 'hippo pool' in the upper reaches of the Savuti Channel near the Selinda spillway, we often observed hippos rolling on to their backs as though in a submissive gesture when elephants came to drink (*right*).

Elephants and buffalo make their way across the floodplain towards the Chobe River in the early afternoon (*previous page*).

# OKAVANGO DELTA

To anyone with only the vaguest knowledge of Africa, Okavango is a word loaded with a mystique and draw all of its own. An African paradise and 'jewel of the Kalahari', it is one of the greatest of all inland deltas, a 16 000-square-kilometre, fan-shaped expanse of sparkling waterways, enchanted palm-fringed islands and crystal-clear lagoons. Considered one of the continent's last great unspoiled wildernesses, Botswana's Okavango Delta is populated with a myriad bird and game species, including the greatest land animal, the majestic African elephant *(right)*.

The Delta has two distinct seasons, high water and low. The mid-year high-water flood is a result of torrential rainfall months earlier in the highlands of Angola far to the north. This slowly seeps down to fill the Okavango River, which eventually spills over to renew the parched earth of the Kalahari and fill countless waterways. In recent years the annual flood has been alarmingly low, giving rise to increasing concern that the Delta is shrinking and will perhaps eventually shrivel and die. A fragile, enchanted wilderness, it remains for now a glorious oasis in a land which is otherwise devoid of permanent water.

The northeastern region of the Okavango Delta has been set aside as the Moremi Wildlife Reserve, originally proclaimed a sanctuary by the Tawana people. Although perhaps not as well known as the Chobe National Park or the Okavango itself, Moremi rates as one of the great, unspoiled game parks of Africa. It is estimated that there are over 71 000 elephants in an area incorporating the Okavango Delta and the Chobe National Park to the northeast.

Brandishing his trunk, a lone bull elephant (*opposite*) demonstrates his displeasure at the presence of our noisy, hovering helicopter, an increasingly popular means of sightseeing in the Okavango.

For the region's many elephants, the lush, abundant grazing along Okavango's waterways (*above*) provides an alternative to the harsh browse of the surrounding woodlands and Kalahari sandveld.

Old male elephants often live solitary lives and are usually peaceful unless provoked, but occasionally one may become aggressive and earn itself the title of 'rogue'. Such aggression may have several causes – old age may have caused slight madness, an old injury could be causing constant irritation, or it could merely have bad memories of an encounter or encounters with its greatest foe, man. Generally, however, mock charges such as that portrayed here are intended only to be intimidating to the intruder – not a difficult task for so imposing a creature!

Elephants will feed on coarse reeds and even papyrus (*above*), fodder that is usually unpalatable to most other species but available to them in abundance throughout the Okavango and its surrounding areas.

Although only a tiny fraction of Botswana's estimated 71 500 elephants, perhaps only 10 percent, visit the Delta itself, those that do revel in the sustenance offered by its densely vegetated, palm-studded islands and well grassed floodplains (*right*) that flourish in early summer after the waters have receded.

# QUEST FOR ELEPHANTS

In compiling this book we decided to concentrate on major elephant populations that are readily accessible to, and regularly seen by, visitors to this continent. We wished to show elephants living in their unspoilt environment, where they have occurred naturally over the aeons, and where we hope that they will continue to live reasonably undisturbed in the future.

Our travels led us through some of the most magnificent game parks and wildlife reserves in Africa from Kenya and Tanzania to Zimbabwe, South Africa, Namibia and Botswana. Certain countries were not included because of political and economic instability or uncertainty, all of which are among the major causes of the decimation of Africa's elephant herds, and others because their elephant populations, while possibly stable or even on the increase, were too insignificant to be major attractions. Among the former were Zambia and Zaïre; Malawi and Uganda were among the latter.

Were we to be asked to name our favourite elephant park from our travels, we would be in a quandary, for each has a charm and unique quality of its own. Tanzania's baobab-studded Tarangire National Park proved to be one of Africa's best kept secrets, and Kenya's Amboseli, with its open habitat and Mount Kilimanjaro as its backdrop, is certainly one of the most picturesque, especially from a photographic point of view. Zimbabwe's Mana Pools in the verdant Zambezi Valley or arid Etosha in Namibia, with its large, waterhole-bound and vehicle-tolerant herds, Savuti's concentrations of big bulls, or the spectacular tuskers of Kruger National Park could each claim a special place in our memory. Add to them the massed herds on the flood plains of Botswana's Chobe National Park, the solitary splendour of a lone desert elephant in the dunes of Namibia's

*Okavango encounter, one of many we were privileged to experience.*

Kaokoland, the natural wonder of Ngorongoro Crater, and the rolling softness of Kenya's Masai Mara, in such contrast to the stark, rugged beauty of Samburu National Reserve, with its slender doum palms, long-necked gerenuk, Grevy's zebra and reticulated giraffe. Nor will we forget the arid woodland savannah of Zimbabwe's Hwange National Park, Kenya's Tsavo East and West, and the lush, water's-edge wonderland of Matusadona National Park on the shores of Lake Kariba. To single out any one park would do the others an injustice.

It is unfortunate that several wild corners of the continent had to be omitted from this book. These included Tanzania's under-developed and remote Selous and Ruaha national parks, which contain some of the largest elephant herds left alive in Africa, and Zambia's South Luangwa National Park, which is slowly winning its battle against poaching. Once one of the best places in Africa to observe large elephant herds, it became a desperate killing field with wholesale poaching of large game in the 1980s.

Gonarezhou National Park in the extreme southeast of Zimbabwe suffered heavily during successive droughts in the 1980s and early 1990s and poaching has also taken a serious toll. Indications are, however, that the elephant population is reviving and there are proposals that this park will form part of a 'megapark' incorporating South Africa's Kruger National Park and land inside Mozambique to the east. It was here, during severe drought conditions in 1992, that the technique of elephant family relocation was pioneered, arousing considerable public interest. Over 600 elephants were successfully moved to the nearby Save Conservancy, while 200 elephants were successfully transported to the Madikwe Reserve in South Africa, more than 1 250 kilometres away.

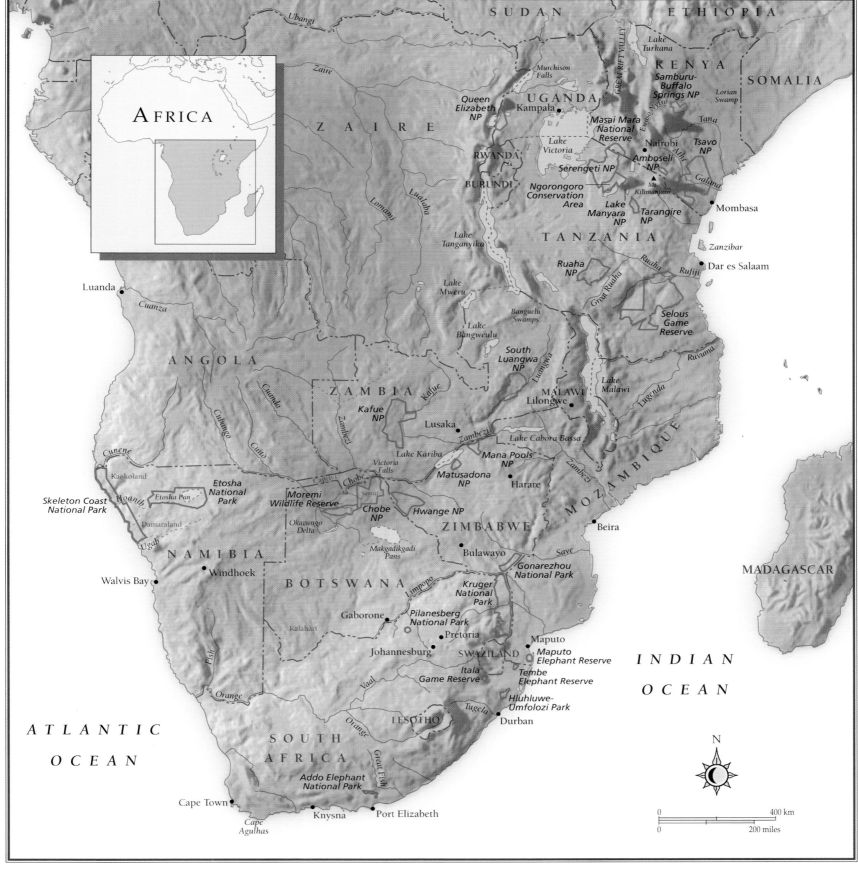

SUDAN

ETHIOPIA

Ubangi

*Zaire*

GREAT RIFT VALLEY

Lake
Turkana

Murchison
Falls

KENYA

SOMALIA

Queen
Elizabeth
NP

UGANDA

Kampala

Samburu-
Buffalo
Springs NP

Lorian
Swamp

ZAIRE

Lualaba

Masai Mara
National
Reserve

Ewaso Nyiro

Tana

RWANDA

Lake
Victoria

Nairobi

Tsavo
NP

Lomami

BURUNDI

Serengeti NP

Amboseli
NP

Galana

Ngorongoro
Conservation
Area

Mt
Kilimanjaro

Mombasa

Lake
Tanganyika

TANZANIA

Lake
Manyara
NP

Tarangire
NP

Zanzibar

Lake
Mweru

Ruaha

Ruaha
NP

Rufiji

Dar es Salaam

Banguelu
Swamps

Great Ruaha

Luanda

Cuanza

Lake
Bangweulu

Selous
Game
Reserve

ANGOLA

South
Luangwa
NP

Ruvuma

Luangwa

Cuando

Cubango

Cuito

ZAMBIA

Kafue

Kafue
NP

MALAWI

Lilongwe

Lake
Malawi

Lugenda

Zambezi

Lusaka

Zambezi

Lake Cabora Bassa

Cunene

Kaokoland

Etosha
National
Park

Caprivi

Chobe

Victoria
Falls

Lake Kariba

Mana Pools
NP

Zambezi

Harare

Matusadona
NP

MOZAMBIQUE

Skeleton Coast
National Park

Hoanib

Etosha Pan

Savuti

Moremi
Wildlife Reserve

Chobe
NP

Hwange NP

Ugab

Damaraland

Okavango
Delta

ZIMBABWE

Beira

NAMIBIA

Makgadikgadi
Pans

Bulawayo

Save

Walvis Bay

Windhoek

BOTSWANA

Gonarezhou
National Park

MADAGASCAR

Limpopo

Kruger
National
Park

Gaborone

Pilanesberg
National Park

Kalahari

Maputo

INDIAN

Fish

Pretoria

Maputo
Elephant Reserve

OCEAN

Johannesburg

SWAZILAND

Tembe
Elephant Reserve

Vaal

Itala
Game Reserve

ATLANTIC

Orange

Hluhluwe-
Umfolozi Park

OCEAN

Orange

Tugela

Durban

LESOTHO

SOUTH
AFRICA

Great Fish

Addo Elephant
National Park

Cape Town

Great Fish

Knysna

Port Elizabeth

Cape
Agulhas

N

0          400 km

0      200 miles

AFRICA

# ACKNOWLEDGMENTS

An undertaking of this scale requires the support of many people and organisations. For four years we travelled through some of Africa's great game parks, seeking out our subjects, and made many new friends who assisted us greatly in their own way. To them, too numerous to mention, a heartfelt thank you.

For permission to work in their parks and reserves, we acknowledge the valuable assistance of the directors and staff of the National Parks Board of South

Africa, the Department of Wildlife and National Parks of Botswana, the Kenya Wildlife Service, the Narok County Council and Isiolo County Council in Kenya (Masai Mara and Samburu national reserves), the Tanzanian National Parks and Ngorongoro Conservation Area Authority, the Namibian Ministry of Conservation and Tourism and the Zimbabwean Department of National Parks and Wildlife Conservation. The kind co-operation, advice and assistance of the staff and officers of these organisations guided us considerably.

We also wish to record our appreciation and gratitude to the authors of the three forewords that add so much to the text of this book, Iain Douglas-Hamilton and Daphne Sheldrick in Kenya and John Hanks in Stellenbosch. Iain also gave of his time and patience to fly us over Tsavo National Park.

The entire text for this book was produced on an IBM Thinkpad 350 Notebook computer, which accompanied us on our travels to some of the most rugged and remote corners of Africa and proved to be an invaluable part of our equipment. We are deeply grateful to Mr Nigel Henzel Thomas of IBM South Africa in Johannesburg for his valued assistance.

In our life and travels as itinerant, nomadic photographers we have frequent need to call upon the hospitality of friends and relatives. Special thanks to Billy and Mich Cochrane in Johannesburg, Joe and Simonne Cheffings in Nairobi, Dave and Samantha Evans in Arusha, David and Cathy Kays in Maun, Jan and Suzi van der Reep in Damaraland, Roger and Stella Howman in Harare, Lloyd and June Wilmot in Savuti, Norman and Mandy MacRitchie in Durban, Anina Conradie in Cape Town, my brother Russell and his wife Lee-Ann in Port Elizabeth, and Mom and Philip in Orapa. We also thank the camps and lodges that have offered us the comfortable alternative of their facilities as a break away from our tents and vehicles: Governor's Camp in the Masai Mara, Amboseli Lodge in Amboseli, Larsen's and Samburu Intrepids in Samburu,

Ngorongoro Crater Lodge in Ngorongoro, Chikwenya Safari Camp in the Zambezi Valley, Fothergill Island Lodge in Matusadona, Huab Safari Lodge and Palmwag Restcamp in Damaraland and Lloyd's Camp in Savuti. For most of the time, however, we enjoyed our solitude in a splendid array of tents supplied by Canvas & Tent, Ladysmith, South Africa. Sharna's parents, Fred and Mo Löffler in Mhlume, Swaziland, continue to offer us shelter and sustenance – and much more – when we come 'home' from the bush.

A special word of thanks to Marie Torlage for her help with the task of mounting, captioning and editing slides! Our photographic problems were professionally solved by South African Nikon agents Hi-Image Distributors (Pty) Ltd, and for their support we thank Brian Schwartz, Dave Aronowitz and Jan Pretorius, along with the technicians who serviced our equipment. Our film was processed by Citylab, Sandton, Johannesburg under the personal supervision of Ezio Beretta and Fazel Kloo – we had not one complaint or problem in the several hundred rolls of film that were developed.

Trappers Trading Company helped clothe us in a selection of their durable outdoor outfits and tough hiking boots, while Safari Centre of Randburg assisted us with the loan of a Magellan Global Positioning System (GPS) for our travels through the remote areas of Damaraland and Kaokoland.

Once again Sean Beneke of SD General Spares (Mananga Tractors), Mhlume, Swaziland assisted in every way in maintaining our vehicles. His generosity and efficiency is hugely appreciated.

Special thanks too to the members of the medical profession who assisted in getting me on my feet again after the Tshokwane episode: Johan Ferreira, Ian Gilbertson, Malcom Funston and David Shein, now in New York.

To Peter Borchert, now editor and publisher of *AFRICA Wildife and Environment* magazine, who gave us the initial encouragement to follow our dream, Neville Poulter and Marje Hemp of Struik Publishers in Cape Town, who gave us the leeway to realise that dream, our sincerest appreciation.

Last, but certainly not least, we wish to record our everlasting gratitude to our parents – without their love, support, enthusiasm and encouragement we would never have achieved all that we have.

DARYL AND SHARNA BALFOUR  Mhlume, Swaziland

# PHOTOGRAPHIC NOTES

Elephants must be among the most photographed animals on earth, for not only are they one of the 'Big Five' and a major tourist attraction in most of Africa's game reserves and national parks, they are also interesting, majestic, endearing, powerful, playful, frightening and awesome – all great photogenic qualities!

Our four-year project photographing elephants for this book could have extended to five, 10, or even more, for, the more you get to know these wonderful beings, the more you realise how little you know. Our task was a labour of love, a fascination that led us on an odyssey over half of Africa. Elephants have long been favourite subjects of ours, and over the years we believe we have developed a rapport that is hard to define. Certainly some of our most satisfying days have been those spent in the dignified company of elephants, usually alone, frequently on foot.

Because of their size, and often their approachability, elephants offer the photographer the opportunity to utilise virtually every lens imaginable, from super-wide-angle to ultra-telephoto. Our battery of Nikon cameras and lenses includes focal lengths ranging from 20 mm right up to 800 mm, and at different times we used them all. However, the lenses we found that we reached for most often were our Nikkor 35–135 mm, 80–200 mm, 300 mm and 500 mm, and we carried these mounted on their own camera bodies, at the ready all the time. Our bodies of choice were the Nikon F4S and F801S, though we also use a totally manual, lightweight FM2, particularly as a back-up when walking long distances. Under all but the most difficult of lighting conditions, we found the built-in Nikon lightmeters infallible and the majority of our shots were taken using matrix metering. We use an incident light meter for calculating exposures when lighting is tricky. Although we set exposures manually much of the time, we have found the Nikon metering and exposure systems almost infallible.

Fujichrome Velvia, exposed at 40 ASA or pushed one stop and exposed at 80 ASA, was our film of choice, and this was professionally processed by the Citylab laboratories in Sandton, Johannesburg. Of many hundreds of rolls of film processed for this project, not one suffered from the intrusions of annoying laboratory gremlins in any way!

Unsteady cameras are the major cause of unsharp photographs, so we always try to rest our cameras on large, heavy 'beanbags' or use a robust tripod with a professional-quality ballhead, more often than not set at its lowest position. For shooting from the vehicle we rest our camera and lens on a beanbag lying on a platform fitted over the windowsill. We have found this method to be far steadier than any special tripod-head attachments made for this purpose.

We keep the use of filters to the absolute minimum, restricting ourselves to polarising and several graduated neutral density options (Singh-Ray), with the very occasional use of an 81B warming filter.

Much of our photography is done on foot, often at considerable distances from where we leave our vehicle, and to facilitate carrying camera equipment over difficult terrain we have modified a large Backpacker Superflight rucksack with a foam cut-out insert into which we can place much of our gear.

The photographs of Tshokwane that appear in this book were, amazingly, recovered unscathed from two Nikon F801S bodies trampled almost beyond recognition during the elephant's attack on me. Despite the crushing attentions of a seven-tonne elephant, neither camera back was sprung and both films were later removed, undamaged, from the mangled remains by the Nikon technicians in Johannesburg. Now that's what we expect from professional equipment! Over the years these same dedicated technicians had become accustomed to us delivering our travel-worn and dusty photographic equipment for servicing and cleaning after yet another expedition into the African wilderness, but this was the worst damage they had encountered. We use Nikon equipment exclusively because it is capable of surviving the knocks and drops inherent in our professional lives.

In the end, however, as with all photography, the essential attributes are knowing your subject, your equipment and, most importantly, just being there! To this end we spend many, many uncomfortable hours in our vehicle, through heat and cold, rain and sunshine, seeking out our subjects or simply remaining with them, on the offchance that something, anything, might happen that we would otherwise miss were we sitting comfortably back in camp. Luck helps, but there can be no substitute for hours put in.

# BIBLIOGRAPHY

**Barbier**, Edward B; Burgess, Joanne C; Swanson, Timothy M, & Pearce, David W (1990) *Elephants, Economics and Ivory.* Earthscan Publications, London.

**Chadwick**, Douglas H (1992) *The Fate of the Elephant.* Penguin Books, London.

**Delort**, Robert (1990) *The Life and Lore of the Elephant.* Thames & Hudson Ltd, London.

**Douglas-Hamilton**, Iain & Oria (1992) *Battle for the Elephants.* Transworld Publishers Ltd, London.

**Eltringham**, Dr S.K. (consultant) (1991) *The Illustrated Encyclopedia of Elephants.* Salamander Books, London.

**Freeman**, Dan (1980) *The Elephant – Endangered Animal.* Bison Books, London.

**Gavron**, Jeremy (1993) *The Last Elephant.* Harper Collins, London.

**Hanks**, John (1979) *A Struggle for Survival.* Struik, Cape Town.

**Kunkel**, Reinhard (1989) *Elephants.* Harry N. Abrams, New York.

**Moss**, Cynthia (1988) *Elephant Memories.* Elm Tree Books, London.

**Moss**, Cynthia, & Colbeck, Martyn (1992) *Echo of the Elephants.* BBC Books, London.

**Potgieter**, De Wet (1995) *Contraband: South Africa and the International Trade in Ivory and Rhino Horn.* Queillerie, Cape Town.

**Redmond**, Ian (1990) *The Elephant Book.* Walker Books, London.

**Streak**, Diana (1994) *Elephants may go on the pill;* Sunday Times, Johannesburg, November 13, 1994.

**Trevor**, Simon (1990) *The Elephants of Tsavo: Love & Betrayal.* Film; Anglia Television, London.

**Trevor**, Simon (1992) *Keepers of the Kingdom.* Film; Anglia Television, London.

**Van der Merwe**, Nikolaas (1993) *On the trail of ivory.* Custos (special elephant issue) p. 20; National Parks Board of South Africa, Pretoria.